THE IDENTITY MANUAL
Who Am I and What's My Mission in Life?

HELLO
my name is

IVAN ROMAN

THE IDENTITY MANUAL

Who Am I and What's My Mission in Life?

HELLO
My Name Is

And This Is My Book

IVAN ROMAN

ENDORSEMENTS

Ivan Roman is a fine young man with a powerful grace and gift from God. You will be greatly helped by his insights and blessed by his book. I encourage you to not just to read it but apply its truths to your daily walk with Christ.

Bobby Conner
Eagle's View Ministries

Without question, we live in the greatest hour of history. God is on the move in the nations of the earth as the church is awakened, souls are saved, and society is transformed. Revival is being ignited in nations across the globe and God's glory is arising on His people. Christians are being called to partner with the Holy Spirit in total abandonment to see God's glory cover the earth. Ivan Roman is a man anointed to call Believers to move with God for revival. Ivan carries a message that is not only revelatory, but activates those hungry to be used by God. This message is not just a theory lacking substance, but was birthed out of personal encounters with the Lord and walked out in the local church. If you long to go deeper with God and be activated to take your place in the greatest revival in history then this book is for you.

Banning Liebscher
Jesus Culture, Bethel Church – Redding, California

What a great book! Ivan has captured the deepest keys to a supernatural life – friendship with God, identity in God, and confidence before God based on sonship. With these foundations firmly established in the heart, healings and miracles become a normal part of life. My prayer is that everyone who reads this book learns to develop the heart that Ivan has for the fullness of life with God.

Stacey Campbell
www.beahero.org
www.revivalnow.com

This new book by Ivan Roman invites us to understand our role as sons and daughters of the Kingdom of God. I have known Ivan for several years and have personally come to know and experience the revelation and substance of heaven that he carries on his life. Within this manual you will not only receive fantastic, forerunning revelation about your position and place as priests and kings in the earth, but you will also receive an impartation of the very nature of God! Ivan Roman is called to reveal, teach and break the body of Christ into something fresh and glorious and this book provides you with the valuable tools necessary to break you into a fresh new season in God!

Jeff Jansen
Founder of Global Fire Ministries International &
Global Fire Church & World Miracle Center & Kingdom Life Institute - Nashville, TN
Author of Glory Rising

In this manual Ivan shares powerful keys that will help you to experience God's presence in a greater measure and also will impart faith for believing God for the impossible. It is a must read for everyone who desires more of God!

Kelry Green

Nearly a decade ago Ivan Roman introduced me to the power of God, the prophetic ministry and living in the supernatural. We spent hours conversing about church history and studying the Word. Joining him on ministry trips I saw the sick healed, the demonized delivered and revival and renewal break out. Nevertheless, the greatest thing I learned from Ivan, the message He lives and breathes, is what you're about to read in this manual—it's a message of intimacy, sonship and identity. Laced with every miracle was a message of intimacy. Found within every prophecy was the heart of the Father. It's becoming so obvious to most of us that this generation needs more than a little religion on Sunday morning and Wednesday night. If we're really going to see global transformation and world harvest, it will undoubtedly be by the hearts and hands of a generation of sons and daughters who have been mentored and esteemed by leaders who carry the love of the Father and wholeheartedly embrace "On earth as it is in heaven." I know this message you're about to read will change your life as much as it has changed mine.

Eric Green
Cofounder & Overseer, Kingdom Life Institute
Global Fire Church & World Miracle Center, Murfreesboro / Nashville, TN
www.ericgreen.org

FORWARD by Denny Cline

If you only read books of statistics about the church in North America and the opinions of those collecting them, you would think the church is finished or at least is completely ineffective. While it is true that the western church is behind in church growth from new conversions compared to other continents, there is real life in the western church. We are advancing in both knowledge and demonstration of the kingdom of God. There have been outpourings of the Holy Spirit that have and are still going around the world giving life to missions and the church at large. You only have to look at what *Global Awakening, The TACF Church, Bethel Church* in Redding, California, and ministries like *Iris* in Africa are doing to see massive impact. The prayer movements and the rebirth of *Youth With A Mission, Young Life,* and all kinds of new church plants and even mega churches all show us that something is stirring. There are saints everywhere in North America going into the market place to pray for the sick, serve the poor, prophesy, and reach out to world.

As I look at the emerging leaders in the age group of young adults I am very optimistic. In fact, I believe we are on the verge of another awakening in our nation and a time like the early 70's when what folks referred to as the "Jesus Movement" broke out bringing many sons and daughters into the kingdom and the church. I was one of those. And many of us "gray hairs" are now leaders in the body of Christ of churches, ministries and evangelistic efforts. Jesus is still building His church and in North America, too.

What Ivan Roman has written in *The Identity Manual* is basic, needed, and profound for any age group. This is just the kind of stuff new converts and those who may have forgotten the basics need. I like both the purpose and flow of this book as well as its utility. Those who read it will also find it useful as a study or teaching tool for groups or ministry training, as well as fun to read as it is filled with stories and insights.

It starts in the right place with understanding of who we are in Christ. One of our past failures in the church has been to either just give knowledge that does not lead to practice or be task oriented without an understanding of the amazing relationship with God that ministry should flow from. This book speaks to both of those values. But it is also more than just information or an equipping tool.

I know Ivan well and appreciate his passion for the kingdom and for living a life that glorifies Jesus and builds family. This book has good foundational teaching, but is also filled with revelation and wisdom. For example: Most of what people say about Enoch is about the idea of walking with God so closely that one day you are just taken up into glory. I like that part. But Ivan caught my attention when he also from just one passage of Scripture gives the insight that Enoch was also a father with a family not just a mystic! That's great stuff. You will find lots of it in this book. I encourage you to both enjoy and use this manual to help equip the church to reach higher and fight the good fight of faith. This book, and its author, is one of the reasons I feel certain the church in North America is on the rise.

Denny Cline
Senior Leader of *Jesus Pursuit Church* and Founder of *Elisha Rising* in Albany, Oregon

INTRODUCTION

"It was he who gave some to be apostles, some to be prophets, some to be evangelists, and some to be pastors and teachers, to prepare God's people for works of service, so that the body of Christ may be built up until we all reach unity in the faith and in the knowledge of the Son of God and become mature, attaining to the whole measure of the fullness of Christ" (Eph. 4:11-13).

The fivefold ministry is for equipping the saints to do the work of the ministry. One word that stands out to me in this passage of Scripture is "some." Jesus' message wasn't only to some—His message was to all. In Mark 16 Jesus says, "And these signs will accompany those who believe...." The ministry of Jesus is to all who believe. Before Jesus sent out His apostles in Matthew 10, He first called them to Himself as disciples. We are called to be disciples and followers of Christ. In John 14:12 Jesus said, *"Most assuredly, I say to you, he who believes in Me, the works that I do he will do also; and greater works than these he will do, because I go to My Father."* Who will do greater works? He who believes.

While Jesus walked the earth He told us the harvest was plentiful but the laborers were few. It is still the same today. God is pouring out His Spirit upon His people—mothers, fathers, and youth—regardless of age, education, wealth, or occupation. God will always have His leaders, but ministry was never intended to be for an elite few. Ministry is a lifestyle for everybody. This manual is for training and equipping everyday believers in understanding their role in this end-time army—the body of Christ.

-Ivan Roman

Part 1
Intimacy, Identity, and Destiny

HELLO
My Name Is

Chapter One

Walking With God

During dinner recently, I heard the voice of the Lord say in my spirit, "Who are they? They prophesy like prophets. They love the lost like evangelists. They heal like healers." Then I heard the Lord say, "They are My sons and daughters." One of the most important messages in this hour is the message of sonship. Before we can walk in the fullness of our destiny we must have the revelation of *who* we are and *whose* we are. This last-days outpouring is not for superstars, but for sons and daughters.

> *"And it shall come to pass afterward that I will pour out My Spirit on all flesh; your sons and your daughters shall prophesy, your old men shall dream dreams, your young men shall see visions"* (Joel 2:28).

In prayer recently I asked the Lord, "What does a manifest son of God look like?" I heard the Lord say, "Enoch." I began to study the life of Enoch, and although there is not a lot about him in Scripture, there is enough to inspire us to be supernaturally natural. As Christians we shouldn't separate who we are from what we do—we are children of God; everything we do in life should flow from this place. We are called the temple of the Holy Spirit; we are carriers of the glory of God. On the cross Jesus' last words were, *"...It is finished"* (John 19:30). In the Greek that phrase literally means *paid in full*. Paid in full was a term used in Christ's day in the marketplace. The work of the cross must be released into the marketplace instead of being limited to a good church service. Christianity was never intended to be an event, but a lifestyle. As we peer into the life of Enoch with fresh eyes, we will understand more clearly our role in this life: to walk with God as His sons and daughters.

One of the few things noted about Enoch in Scripture is that he *"...walked with God..."* (Gen. 5:24). I believe Enoch's greatest endeavor was to walk with the Most High. Fellowshipping with the Lord was His greatest passion. This is a great contrast and warning to many today. Success in the kingdom is not how well known we are on earth. I heard Bill Johnson, Pastor of Bethel Church in Redding, California once say, "We are to be known in Heaven and feared in hell." Friendship with God—walking with God—is what matters at the end of the day. How well we know God should be the pursuit of every believer. Our identity should never be found in what we do for a living, or even in what we do for God. Our identity must spring from our relationship with our Father.

> *"And Enoch walked with God; and he was not, for God took him"* (Gen. 5:24).

The word *walked* in the Hebrew is *halak*, which means *to walk up and down*. The understanding is Enoch had numerous visitations into heaven. We are in a season where the door of Revelation 4:1 has been opened and the invitation is still the same, *"...come up here."* This statement may be very controversial, but the Lord is raising up people that live in the reality that heaven is their home *now*. There will be such a revelation of this that, like David, we will say, *"I am a stranger on the earth..."* (Ps. 119:19).

> *"These all died in faith, not having received the promises, but having seen them afar off were assured of them, embraced them and confessed that they were strangers and pilgrims on the earth. For those who say such things declare plainly that they seek a homeland. And truly if they had called to mind that country from which they had come out, they would have had opportunity to return. But now they desire a better, that is, a heavenly country. Therefore God is not ashamed to be called their God, for He has prepared a city for them"* (Heb. 11:13-16).

My prayer has been that the Lord would allow me to peer into heaven and have a glimpse of eternity—my real home. When the reality of eternity touches our hearts we won't hold on to temporal things the way we do. God is raising up a company of people that possess the heart of Enoch. To walk with God in the supernatural, to fall so in love with heaven that God says, "Since you are here so much, why don't you just stay?" People that have a heavenly eternal perspective behave and speak differently like the mystics of old; they stand out from the rest of society. In the midst of busyness, the scripture says to *"Be still, and know that I am God"* (Ps. 46:10). I encourage you to learn to find stillness in any environment. As a traveling minister, I have found it necessary to treasure moments of silence, whether it be in a busy airport, or on a crowded plane. In the midst of noise I can find quiet in my heart. In doing this I'm not reaching out to a God that is somewhere off in the expanse, but to my Father and Friend who dwells in me. A genuine relationship with God inspires people around us; not with mere doctrine, but with passion—a real knowing of God.

"Enoch lived sixty-five years, and begot Methuselah" (Gen. 5:21).

We see from this scripture that Enoch had a child, so we can speculate that he had a wife. We read in Jude that he was a prophet (see verse 14). Enoch wasn't hiding off in the caves somewhere. He had responsibilities as a father and a husband and yet he was able to find time to walk with his God. Enoch's life is to be an example to us of a lifestyle of prayer and the supernatural, not merely listening to the Spirit in a Christian setting, but walking in the Spirit—in a continual attitude of prayer with one ear toward heaven. Isaiah 50 says that the Lord awakens our ears morning by morning. Continual communion with God is possible, and it's desired by the Father. The most common excuse in North America is, "I don't have time." The thing that the Lord desires of us *is* our time! In Revelation 3:18 Jesus says to come buy from Him gold refined in the fire. It is interesting that Jesus says to *buy* from Him. The question then is, "What is the price of the gold?" A friend of mine asked the Lord this question. The Lord responded, "Your life, but I'll take your time for now." According to Matthew 6:6, it's very important to go into a secret place to pray to have alone time with God.

Smith Wigglesworth is quoted as saying, "I don't pray more than 15 minutes, but I don't go more than 15 minutes without praying." When the understanding of prayer becomes more about fellowshipping with our God—Father and Friend—it will no longer be our duty as Christians, but a privilege and the longing desire of our hearts. Modern technology is awesome, but it can be a great distraction from the simplicity of devotion to God.

Lastly, Enoch means *dedicated* or *consecrated*. If we desire to walk with God like Enoch walked, we must be willing to allow the Holy Spirit to set us apart. I had a dream recently where a man I recognize as a prophetic voice said to me, "Do you want to know the keys to visitation?" He said, "Who may ascend the hill of the Lord?" Immediately in my spirit I heard, "He who has clean hands and a pure heart." Then the man looked at me and said, "In quietness and stillness." As we quiet ourselves before God, and wait in His presence, His Holy Spirit will begin to release His very nature into our beings. Holiness is not a bad word. Holiness is to be like Christ. Holiness is not about what you do or don't do—it's not a set of rules. Out of our relationship with God we begin to learn what He loves and hates; then we choose because of love to do the things He loves.

As we learn to rest in the presence of God, His manifest glory will begin to remain upon us. The leaders in Jerusalem perceived that Peter and John were uneducated and untrained men, but marveled when they heard them speak—they knew they had been with Jesus (see Acts 4:13). When we spend time with Jesus, His presence stays with us. The angels love the presence of God, and if you are a carrier, they are surrounding you as well. People who walk with God change atmospheres wherever they go, at *their* mere presence. In the book of Acts it says people laid the sick out on mats so that Peter's shadow could touch them, and they would be healed.

Charles Finney once walked into a factory and the workers fell to their knees crying out, "What must we do to be saved?" The reality of the presence and glory of God is being released to the Church. Our eyes are opening to see how the light of God's glory dwelling in us affects the world around us.

> *"To them God willed to make known what are the riches of the glory of this mystery among the Gentiles: which is Christ in you, the hope of glory"* (Col. 1:27).

Enoch is a type of a manifest or mature son of God. His life shows us that in the midst of having responsibilities (children or work) he was still able to walk with God in deep communion. God is calling us to walk with Him—to be supernaturally natural—having our heads in the heavens and our feet on the earth, walking out His plans.

The life of Enoch teaches us many things: to find our success in being a friend of God, to live a life where the presence of God is cherished above any earthly treasure, and that heaven is our home now. Know that when we walk with God, His desires become our desires and His likes become our likes. I've heard the invitation to come up here, and to that I say, "Yes, Lord!"

Reflection Questions

1. Explain in your own words what it means to walk with God.

_____

_____

_____

_____

_____

2. What happens if we practice Psalms 46:10?

_____

_____

_____

_____

_____

3. What does it mean to be consecrated to the Lord and why is it important?

_____

_____

_____

_____

_____

- NOTES -

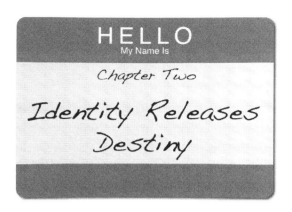

HELLO
My Name Is

Chapter Two

Identity Releases Destiny

If you were to ask someone today who they are, most would reply by stating their job title, their race, or how they feel about themselves. You would hear, "I'm a doctor," "I'm an American," or "I'm a loser." Our identity is not to be found in any of these, only in being a son or daughter of God. I've heard prophetic teacher Bobby Conner say, "Heaven and hell are asking the same question, 'Who do you think you are?'" In Matthew 16:14-19 we see Jesus asking a question to Peter, *"Who do you say I am?"*

> *"When Jesus came to the region of Caesarea Philippi, he asked his disciples, 'Who do people say the Son of Man is?' They replied, 'Some say John the Baptist; others say Elijah; and still others, Jeremiah or one of the prophets.' 'But what about you?' he asked. 'Who do you say I am?' Simon Peter answered, 'You are the Christ, the Son of the living God.' Jesus replied, 'Blessed are you, Simon son of Jonah, for this was not revealed to you by man, but by my Father in heaven. And I tell you that you are Peter, and on this rock I will build my church, and the gates of Hades will not overcome it. I will give you the keys of the kingdom of heaven; whatever you bind on earth will be bound in heaven, and whatever you loose on earth will be loosed in heaven'"* (Matt. 16:14-19).

Peter has a revelation from God who Jesus is, the Son of the living God. Jesus, in return, reveals to Peter who Peter himself is called to be. As we spend time with Jesus and dig into His Word, the Holy Spirit reveals to us who He is and who we are in Him. There is *no* other way to walk in our true identities as children of God. In the world we gain acceptance from people by the things we accomplish, thus finding our identity in what we do; this is not the way in the kingdom. In the kingdom of God we are accepted and loved no matter the circumstances, and from that we yearn to do good works. Performance based acceptance seems to be a huge issue in our society. It starts with little children, "Daddy, look how fast I can run." Subconsciously we learn that people love us because of what we do. God loves us whether we are raising the dead or taking a nap.

> *"When all the people were being baptized, Jesus was baptized too. And as he was praying, heaven was opened and the Holy Spirit descended on him in bodily form like a dove. And a voice came from heaven: 'You are my Son, whom I love; with you I am well pleased'"* (Luke 3:21-22).

I have always been amazed by this scripture. Jesus, up until this point in His life, had performed no miracles. God was pleased with Jesus not because of all the miracles, but because He was His Son. This is the first key in understanding our authority as believers. Jesus says to His disciples before leaving, *"I will not leave you as orphans"* (John 14:18). Prior to coming to Christ, our original state is as orphans; that's why in Romans 8:15 the Spirit of adoption causes us to cry out *"Abba, Father.'"* We have been adopted into the family of God by our heavenly Father, according to Romans 8, and in this become His children. The Bible says we have become heirs of God and co-heirs with Christ Jesus (see Rom. 8:17). In order for us to walk in our given authority, we must have an understanding of *who* we are and *whose* we are. The devil is afraid of believers who know who they are in Christ. He will try to keep us from understanding our identity as sons and daughters of God.

Immediately after the Father affirms Jesus as His Son, the Holy Spirit leads Him into the wilderness to be tempted by the devil. It is very interesting to see how the enemy tempts Jesus. Two times Satan says to Jesus, *"If you really are the son of God"* (Matt. 4:3, 6). Satan is challenging Jesus' identity as a Son. This is the same exact battle we are in; it's the battle over our identity. In order for us to operate in the authority Christ has given us, we must understand who we are. Our faith in Jesus Christ enables us to overcome the world. A six-year-old child who has faith in Jesus Christ has more power than any devil in hell.

In the movie, *Lion King,* there is a scene where Simba looks into his reflection in the water and see His father. The monkey says what do you see? The sky opens up and Simba sees His father, the King, in the clouds. King Mufasa says, "You have forgotten me." Simba replies, "How have I forgotten you?" Mufasa says, "Because you have forgotten who you are." Simba was the son of the King, the heir to the throne. He was living a carefree life, hakuna matata, no worries. Until he realized he had a mandate to restore his father's kingdom. As believers if we wander around not knowing who we are, we won't ever step into our Kingdom mandate. As sons and daughters of the King, we are called to manifest his Kingdom with signs, wonders, and miracles.

After Jesus overcomes Satan in the wilderness we read, *"Jesus returned to Galilee in the power of the Spirit, and news about him spread through the whole countryside. He taught in their synagogues, and everyone praised him"* (Luke 4:14-15). Jesus returned from the wilderness in the *power of the Spirit*—signs, wonders, and miracles followed His ministry. As believers we have seasons that feel like we are in the wilderness. Those are the seasons where the enemy challenges our identity. As we stand on the word that we are God's beloved children in whom He is well pleased, our ministries and callings are solidified from that place. There is nothing we can do to gain God's love and acceptance; it comes simply because while we were yet sinners Christ died on the Cross for us (see Rom. 5:8). Value is determined by how much someone is willing to pay for something. Jesus purchased us with His own blood.

> *"David said, 'My son Solomon is young and inexperienced, and the house to be built for the LORD should be of great magnificence and fame and splendor in the sight of all the nations. Therefore I will make preparations for it.' So David made extensive preparations before his death"* (1 Chron. 22:5).

> *"'I have taken great pains to provide for the temple of the LORD a hundred thousand talents of gold, a million talents of silver, quantities of bronze and iron too great to be weighed, and wood and stone. And you may add to them. You have many workmen: stonecutters, masons and carpenters, as well as men skilled in every kind of work in gold and silver, bronze and iron—craftsmen beyond number. Now begin the work, and the LORD be with you'"* (1 Chron. 22:14-16).

Let's break down the cost of building this temple:

-100,000 talents of gold are equivalent today to 3,750 tons of gold.

-1,000,000 talents of silver are equivalent to 37,500 tons.

-This totals 41,250 tons of precious metal.

-Quantities of bronze and iron too great to be weighed.

-Including wood and stone.

The incredible thing about this is we are the temple of the Holy Ghost (see 1 Cor. 6:19). The dwelling place of God is us. Jesus paid a greater price for us than David paid for Solomon's temple. If you ever feel like you have no value, just remember the price Jesus paid for you.

Reflection Questions

1. At the time when Jesus was baptized and the Father spoke from heaven, "You are my Son, whom I love; with you I am well pleased," how many miracles had Jesus done in His life? How many demons did he cast out?

_____

_____

_____

_____

_____

2. What was the Father pleased with?

_____

_____

_____

_____

_____

3. What is the key to walking in our God-given destinies?

_____

_____

_____

_____

_____

4. How is value determined?

_____

_____

_____

_____

_____

- NOTES -

HELLO
My Name Is

Chapter Three

God Confidence

The Spirit Himself bears witness with our spirit that we are children of God, and if children, then heirs—heirs of God and joint heirs with Christ, if indeed we suffer with Him, that we may also be glorified together (Rom. 8:16-17).

Being sons and daughters of God is an incredible honor. We have not only been saved from eternal separation from God, but we have been adopted into the family of God. As we join this family, all that belongs to God belongs to us. Wow! What an amazing thought. A synonym for the word *grace* is *God's riches at Christ's expense*. Because Jesus died on the cross, everything He died for is available to us. Once in prayer I heard the Father say, "I desire that my Son receive the reward of His sufferings." The reward for His sufferings is that the world He died for would walk in close relationship with the Father, and by faith walk in their inheritance. We can settle for nothing less than the fullness, for His sake. Jesus was crucified for the forgiveness of our sins so that we could have eternal life in heaven, but also so we could have abundant life now, here on earth (see John 10:10).

We should not be living like beggars, but like royalty; we are sons and daughters of the King. The Lord desires to remove the slave mindset which is produced from the orphan spirit. Traveling to third world countries I have seen my share of orphans; but I've never had an orphan on the streets walk up to me and ask, "Can you hold me?" They normally ask for money or food. God's children are no longer orphans or slaves (see Rom. 8:15; John 15:15). God's people should always have servant's hearts, but that is very different from the mindset of a slave. Jesus was the greatest servant that ever lived, and we should have the same attitude He had.

"Your attitude should be the same as that of Christ Jesus: Who, being in very nature God, did not consider equality with God something to be grasped, but made himself nothing, taking the very nature of a servant, being made in human likeness. And being found in appearance as a man, he humbled himself and became obedient to death—even death on a cross" (Phil. 2:5-8)!

The heart to serve people is what ministry is all about. There is a difference between slaves and bondservants. In Bible times, after a slave served his master for seven years he was given the choice of whether he wanted to continue to work or to leave. If the servant decided to stay the master would take the ear of the servant and pierce it against a door. The servant was then the property of the master and became a bondservant. The difference is simply that the bondservant is now a part of the family and chose to serve the master out of sheer love rather than being required to.

"If a fellow Hebrew, a man or a woman, sells himself to you and serves you six years, in the seventh year you must let him go free. And when you release him, do not send him away empty-handed. Supply him liberally from your flock, your threshing floor and your winepress. Give to him as the LORD your God has blessed you. Remember that you were slaves in Egypt and the Lord your God redeemed you. That is why I give you this command today. But if your servant says to you, 'I do not want to leave you,' because he loves you and your family and is well off with you, then take an awl and push it through his ear lobe into the door, and he will become your servant for life. Do the same for your maidservant" (Deut. 15:12-17).

Peter, Paul, James, Jude, and John call themselves bondservants of Jesus Christ.

"Simon Peter, a bondservant and apostle of Jesus Christ..." (2 Peter 1:1 NKJV).

"Paul, a bondservant of Jesus Christ, called to be an apostle, separated to the gospel of God..." (Rom. 1:1 NKJV).

"James, a bondservant of God and of the Lord Jesus Christ..." (James 1:1 NKJV).

"Jude, a bondservant of Jesus Christ, and brother of James..." (Jude 1:1 NKJV).

"The Revelation of Jesus Christ, which God gave Him to show His servants— things which must shortly take place. And He sent and signified it by His angel to His servant (doulos—bondservant) John..." (Rev. 1:1 NKJV).

Christians are called to be *love-slaves* of Jesus, those who serve Him out of a deep love and affection. When Abraham was old, he sent his bondservant to find a wife for his son Isaac. This was a huge responsibility (see Gen. 24:1-4). As we position our hearts to serve the Lord in humility, He begins to entrust us with greater levels of authority. Jesus humbled Himself, and as a result God highly exalted Him (see Phil. 2:8-9). It's our job to humble ourselves and God does the exalting—if we do His job, then He'll do ours. Being a love-slave doesn't take away the fact that we are sons and daughters. We come to God as sons who serve out of deep love; we face the world as ambassadors. An ambassador represents another country in power and authority. We are called to represent Christ to those who don't know Him. The Lord desires us to have the revelation of how much He loves us and how much He wants to demonstrate His love and power through us. Having confidence in ourselves is important, but not nearly as important as confidence in God. I can imagine what the people thought when they heard Peter say, *"Silver or gold I do not have, but what I have I give you."* You see, Peter knew what he had; he says it in the next line, *"In the name of Jesus Christ of Nazareth, walk"* (Acts 3:6). It is true that without Christ we can do nothing, but with Christ all things are possible.

The apostle Paul writes a letter to the church of Corinth and calls them saints. Then, later in the letter, Paul goes on to address the awful sin that is taking place among them. Revelation 1:6 says that we are a royal race—we should no longer find our identity in being sinners, but as saints. Becoming a Christian doesn't make us better than anyone; it only reveals that we have realized our desperate need for Him. *""For in him we live and move and have our being"""* (Acts 17:28). Asking Jesus to become our Lord and Savior is an incredible sign of humility—confessing that we can't live our lives without Him.

Here is a definition of humility from The New Unger's Bible Dictionary:

HUMILITY (Heb. `anawa, "gentleness, affliction," also from `ana, "to be bowed down"; Grk. tapeinophrosune, "lowliness of mind," praotes, "gentleness"). Humility in the spiritual sense is an inwrought grace of the soul that allows one to think of himself no more highly than he ought to think (Eph. 4:1-2; Col. 3:12-13; cf. Rom. 12:3). In contrast, the moralists considered humility (from humus, "earth") to be meanness of spirit. The exercises of it are first and chiefly toward God (Matt. 11:29; James 1:21). It requires us to feel that in God's sight we have no merit and to in honor prefer others to ourselves (Rom. 12:10; cf. Prov. 15:33). It does not demand undue self-depreciation but rather lowliness of self-estimation and freedom from vanity. The Gk. term praotes, "gentleness" (rendered "meekness" in KJV) expresses a spirit of willingness and obedience and a lack of resistance to God's dealings with us. But humility must also be expressed towards those who wrong us, in order that their insults and wrongdoing might be used by God for our benefit (see Acts 20:18-21). It is enjoined of God (Ps. 25:9; Col. 3:12; James 4:6,10) and is essential to discipleship under Christ (Matt. 18:3-4).

BIBLIOGRAPHY: R. C. Trench, Synonyms of the New Testament (1953), pp. 148-57.
(From The New Unger's Bible Dictionary. Originally published by Moody Press of Chicago, Illinois. Copyright © 1988.)

One of the greatest signs of humility is a life of prayer and obedience to God. The greatest sign of pride is disobedience. When we live a lifestyle of prayer and radical obedience, we are showing by our actions that we need Jesus just to get through the day.

"Now Moses was a very humble man, more humble than anyone else on the face of the earth" (Num. 12:3).

This scripture has always made me chuckle on the inside. Moses was the author of the first five books of the Bible. I can imagine the Holy Spirit whispering to Moses, "Hey, write this, 'Moses was the most humble man on the face of the earth.'" Who me? What is the lesson we need to learn from this? You are who God says you are; nothing more and nothing less. If God says you are a king, humility is leaning on God to be king. Remember when God called Saul king and he hid in the baggage during his coronation? That was a huge sign of Saul's pride and false humility. True humility says, "God, I can't do it without You, but if You say I am, then let me become it." Later in the story a young boy named David acted completely opposite than Saul had previously acted. When David faced Goliath, he appeared to those around him prideful and arrogant—a young boy thinking he could take on a giant. David wasn't confident in his ability as much as He was confident in God's ability.

> *"The LORD who delivered me from the paw of the lion and the paw of the bear will deliver me from the hand of this Philistine"* (1 Sam. 17:37).

The Lord desires to bring His church to a place of walking in greater works than He even did while on earth (see John 14:12). It's not self-confidence that we're after, but God-confidence—knowing who it is that loves us, and how much He paid for us to walk in His power and love.

> *"From the days of John the Baptist until now, the kingdom of heaven has been forcefully advancing, and forceful men lay hold of it"* (Matt. 11:12).

God's children must be tenacious and contend for everything He has for us. Settling for less than all He has for us is not humility—it's pride. By our actions, we show that we don't need Him if we're not willing to fight for and receive all that He has called us to walk in.

There are people in the church today that have served the Lord for years, never departing from their faith, but who feel enslaved. They have no delight in serving the Lord. They faithfully attend every service, hold steady to their daily disciplines of prayer and Bible reading, but have no joy in their hearts. How can this be? I call this the older brother syndrome.

Remember the story of the prodigal son? The younger son asks his father for his inheritance early. He wastes it on partying and other meaningless things. Then, when he returns home, the Father runs to him, throws him a party, gives him a ring, a cloak, sandals, and kills a fattened calf! The older brother gets jealous. He says that he has served his father faithfully for years and never had a party. The Father responds by saying that everything in the house belongs to the older son and he would have thrown him a party the whole time if he would have only asked (see Luke 15:11-21).

It is very possible for us to walk around the Father's house, where there is a buffet set before us, and get full on the appetizers. I want to eat everything on the table. I want the Father to throw a party for me now. I want anointing, inheritances, and everything that belongs to Jesus since we are joint-heirs. Understanding our identity as sons and daughters helps us understand our function in the body of Christ. Understanding our position as sons and daughters of God gives us a revelation of our function as prophets, priests, and kings. In the following chapters we will discover the threefold ministry of every believer: prophet, priest, and king.

Reflection Questions

1. What is the difference between having the heart of a servant and the mindset of a slave?

_____

_____

_____

_____

_____

2. What is the synonym for grace that we talked about in this chapter? What do you think about it?

_____

_____

_____

_____

_____

3. Mediate by yourself, or share in a group setting, your thoughts on desiring the fullness. List your thoughts below.

_____

_____

_____

_____

_____

- NOTES -

Part 2

Prophet, Priest, and King

In the Old Testament there were three functions of authority that God used and anointed: prophet, priest, and king. Jesus fulfilled all of them during His earthly ministry. As New Testament believers we are still called to function in these three areas. The prophet hears the voice of God, the priest ministers to the Lord, and the king rules and reigns. In the following chapters we will look at, in more detail, each of these functions individually, and how they relate to the believer's life today.

HELLO
My Name Is

Chapter Four

The Believer and The Prophet

Are all apostles? Are all prophets?
Are all teachers? Do all work miracles? Do all have gifts of healing? Do all
speak in tongues? Do all interpret? But eagerly desire the greater gifts
(1 Cor. 12:29-31).

According to Scripture, not all people are called to be prophets. When I speak on the prophet in this chapter, I am not talking about walking in the role of a New Testament prophet, but being a prophetic generation and developing a lifestyle of hearing the voice of the Shepherd, which is the gift of every believer.

> *"'The watchman opens the gate for him, and the sheep listen to his voice. He calls his own sheep by name and leads them out. When he has brought out all his own, he goes on ahead of them, and his sheep follow him because they know his voice. But they will never follow a stranger; in fact, they will run away from him because they do not recognize a stranger's voice'"* (1 John 10:2-5).

We are all called to hear the voice of God. *"It is written: "Man does not live on bread alone, but on every word that comes from the mouth of God""* (Matt. 4:4). We are all called to hear God's voice out of intimacy with Him. God's voice brings us affirmation, love, guidance, direction, vision, revelation, and sanctification. Hearing the voice of God requires spending time with Him in stillness and quietness. There are many ways God speaks to us; we must learn to spend time with Him which will enable us to discern His voice from our own. Hearing the voice of God should be the yearning desire of every believer's heart. One of the phrases recorded most out of the lips of the Lord Jesus were, *"He who has an ear, let him hear what the Spirit says..."* (Rev. 2:7; see also Matthew 13:9; Mark 4:23; Luke 8:8). It's essential that we hear what the Lord is speaking to us today.

God's Voice Brings Direction and Guidance

"Today, if you hear his voice, do not harden your hearts" (Heb. 4:7).

I have learned to cherish the Lord's voice in my life; I don't know how I would live without it. One recent account of the voice of the Lord in my life was when the Lord began to speak to me and my wife Erica about moving to Albany, Oregon. One night in a dream my wife said, "Honey, we're moving to Albany." The next morning I told my wife about the dream. Her eyes widened and she said, "The Lord told me yesterday we were going to move to Albany." We drove down to Albany with no job offers or open doors, and out of obedience started looking for a home. Previously we were trying to get a home in another city and no doors opened. Right when we positioned ourselves to move to Albany we received breakthrough. We became qualified for a home, found a great deal on a house, and doors opened for me to teach at a local training center in a wonderful church. The Bible says, *"Those who are led by the Spirit of God are sons of God"* (Rom. 8:14). In the Greek it would appropriately read, "Those who are *governed* by the Spirit are the *mature sons* of God." Hearing and obeying the voice of God in our lives is a sign of maturity.

Jesus is our example of how we are to live life. The book of Isaiah says, *"The Sovereign LORD has given me an instructed tongue, to know the word that sustains the weary. He wakens me morning by morning, wakens my ear to listen like one being taught"* (Isa. 50:4). The Lord Jesus heard the voice of His Father every morning. Another scripture that shows us the frequency of the Father's voice in Jesus' life is John 5:19—*"Jesus gave them this answer: 'I tell you the truth, the Son can do nothing by himself; he can do only what he sees his Father doing, because whatever the Father does the Son also does.'"* Jesus couldn't see what the Father was doing without hearing His voice.

God is our Father and He desires to speak to us. Relationship is what this thing called Christianity is all about. I have experienced the Father's voice in my marriage as well. The Lord once spoke to me and said that my wife was having a hard day and I should buy her roses. I came home with the roses and she said, "Thank you, I needed that; I had a really hard day." I love my Abba Father so much; His voice has led me into blessings and out of potential danger. Moses cried out in Numbers 11:29 that He wished that all the Lord's people were prophets and that the Lord would put His Spirit on them. Moses' didn't actually desire that all of God's people would function as prophets, but that all of God's people would learn to hear His voice for themselves. This is still God's desire today.

God's Voice Releases Revelation

Proverbs 29:18 states, *"Where there is no revelation, the people cast off restraint...."* The picture here is a group of horses in a corral wandering around in circles with no place to go. Horses that have been corralled for a long time get bored and often start fighting with each other. If there is a lack of prophetic revelation in our lives we will wander aimlessly, often being led off course.

King David is a good example of what happens when God's people don't have vision or revelation from the Lord. During the times when kings went out to war, David stayed home. David lost his vision and then saw Bathsheba bathing on the rooftop. He lusted in his heart for her, and in the end committed adultery and murder. We as believers must live by God's revelation or we'll grow apathetic. Scripture says that Jesus endured the cross because of the joy set before Him. All of us have a cross to bear; the only way to carry it is by seeing the joy it will lead us to. The joy set before Jesus was salvation for all who believe. For you it may be a massive harvest of souls, a broken family being restored, or someone delivered from drugs. We persevere through times of difficulty because our eyes are set upon the prize. Remember though, the ultimate prize is knowing the Lord personally. This is what enables us to make it through the hardest of times.

> *"[For my determined purpose is] that I may know Him [that I may progressively become more deeply and intimately acquainted with Him, perceiving and recognizing and understanding the wonders of His Person more strongly and more clearly], and that I may in that same way come to know the power outflowing from His resurrection [which it exerts over believers], and that I may so share His sufferings as to be continually transformed [in spirit into His likeness even] to His death, [in the hope] that*

if possible I may attain to the [spiritual and moral] resurrection [that lifts me] out from among the dead [even while in the body]. Not that I have now attained [this ideal], or have already been made perfect, but I press on to lay hold of (grasp) and make my own, that for which Christ Jesus (the Messiah) has laid hold of me and made me His own. I do not consider, brethren, that I have captured and made it my own [yet]; but one thing I do [it is my one aspiration]: forgetting what lies behind and straining forward to what lies ahead. I press on toward the goal to win the [supreme and heavenly] prize to which God in Christ Jesus is calling us upward." (Phil. 3:12-14 AMP).

Take note Paul says that he forgets the past in order to reach those things that are ahead. If we constantly live in nostalgia and past regrets, it will hinder us from moving forward, robbing us of our God-given destinies. I once heard a man say, "If you try to go back into the past, you'll lose your future." As God's people, we have been given *today* to impact *tomorrow*. One strategy of the enemy is to keep people focused on their past, or living in the *glory days*. Let us heed Paul's admonition and press on toward the goal for the prize of the upward call of God in Christ Jesus.

Discovering Calling

"'For I know the plans I have for you,' declares the LORD, 'plans to prosper you and not to harm you, plans to give you hope and a future'" (Jer. 29:11-12).

We were created to do more than occupy space. One of the most frequent questions I have been asked during my time in ministry is, "What is my calling?" The first key to discovering what we are called to do was mentioned in chapter two, *Identity Releases Destiny*: spending time in the presence of the Lord and listening. Another key to discover God's call on our lives is listening to the desires of our hearts. Early in my walk with God I heard Jeremiah 17:9 quoted, *"The heart is deceitful above all things and beyond cure. Who can understand it?"* I was taught that we can't trust the desires of our hearts because they are wicked. If I ask someone who loves the Lord what the desire of their heart is, they will generally respond with things like revival in their city, or for their family to be saved, or for their friends to come to know Jesus. When we asked Jesus Christ to come and live in our hearts by his Spirit, He changes our desires—He gives us a new heart where He dwells.

> *"I will give you a new heart and put a new spirit in you; I will remove from you your heart of stone and give you a heart of flesh. And I will put my Spirit in you and move you to follow my decrees and be careful to keep my laws"* (Ez. 36:25-27).

These passages of scripture took place in our lives when we were born again.

> *"In reply Jesus declared, 'I tell you the truth, no one can see the kingdom of God unless he is born again.' 'How can a man be born when he is old?' Nicodemus asked. 'Surely he cannot enter a second time into his mother's womb to be born!' Jesus answered, 'I tell you the truth, no one can enter the kingdom of God unless he is born of water and the Spirit'"* (John 3:3-5).

The Bible says in Psalms 37:4 to *"Delight yourself in the LORD and he will give you the desires of your heart."* As we spend quality time with the Lord, we begin to care about the things He cares about. Obviously not every desire is from God, but very often God places a burning desire in our hearts to do something for Him. I would encourage you to cultivate the desires found in your heart. Desires can change with age, but there are those *God-desires* that seem to have been there as long as you can remember. If they are from God they will be motivated by love and produce good fruit. What is the desire of your heart?

A few more keys to discovering your calling are prophetic words and glimpses into the future. If a prophetic word spoken over your life confirms the desire in your heart and has been confirmed by the mouth of two or three witnesses, you should do as Habakkuk 2:2-3 instructs and *"Write down the revelation and make it plain on tablets so that a herald may run with it. For the revelation awaits an appointed time; it speaks of the end and will not prove false. Though it linger, wait for it; it will certainly come and will not delay."* A glimpse into the future is when the Lord allows us to touch our destiny before we are actually called to step into it. If you have the opportunity to go on a mission trip and are ministering to orphans and think to yourself, "I would be happy doing this the rest of my life," you just had a glimpse of your calling. Think back and try to remember times you felt that way—these memories often make you feel joy and purpose.

As I've noted in this chapter, calling is extremely important. But it's also vital that we don't forget to enjoy the journey. Once I took my two-year-old son on a walk to the park. I started to get frustrated because he would stop at every driveway and pick up a rock, or look at a kitty in a window. Then the Lord spoke to my heart and said, "He's enjoying the journey." I have found in my own life that if we are constantly looking for what's going to happen tomorrow, we miss the blessing that can only be found today. Yesterday has past and tomorrow is not yet; the only day we have charge over is today. Enjoy today while it's called today. God will take care of tomorrow.

Reflection Questions

1. How often can we hear the voice of God?

_____

_____

_____

_____

2. What phrase did Jesus say more than any other in the Scripture?

_____

_____

_____

_____

3. What is one thing that can hinder us from moving forward?

_____

_____

_____

_____

_____

4. Why is prophetic revelation so important?

_____

_____

_____

_____

_____

5. What are a few keys mentioned in this chapter that help us discover the call of God on our lives?

_____

_____

_____

_____

_____

_____

- NOTES -

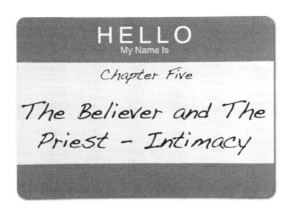

HELLO
My Name Is

Chapter Five

The Believer and The Priest - Intimacy

*I will raise up for myself a faithful priest, who will do according to what is
in my heart and mind. I will firmly establish his house, and he will minister
before my anointed one always* (1 Sam. 2:35).

The purpose of the priesthood is first and foremost to minister to the Lord. The priestly ministry has to be very mindful of this point. It is very easy to be like Martha, always busy ministering to people—although this is very important, it is the second commandment. We must keep the first commandment the first commandment; love the Lord with all your heart, mind, soul and strength. Loving your neighbor as you love yourself is secondary, flowing from the fulfillment of the first commandment. When people put the second commandment first, it leads to burn out and lack of patience and love for people. We were created to worship and fellowship with God.

> *"You yourselves have seen what I did to Egypt, and how I carried you on
> eagles' wings and brought you to myself"* (Ex. 19:4).

Many preachers talk about how God took the children of Israel out of Egypt to bring them into the Promised Land and all of the blessings it contained. This is part of it, but not the biggest part. The above verse says the Lord led Israel out of Egypt to bring them to Himself. It has always been God's intention to fellowship with a people set apart for Himself. The Lord walked with Adam in the cool of the day. God desires to fellowship with man. Adam sinned and man lost communication with God; in response, God, out of His love, sent His Son to die on a cross reconciling us back to Himself. Salvation is unquestionably the greatest miracle, but not the only purpose of salvation according to

John 17:3—*"Now this is eternal life: that they may know you, the only true God, and Jesus Christ, whom you have sent."* Knowing God has become the greatest desire of my life, and I have learned that it is God's greatest desire for us.

> *"This is what the LORD says: 'Let not the wise man boast of his wisdom or the strong man boast of his strength or the rich man boast of his riches, but let him who boasts boast about this: that he understands and knows me'"* (Jer. 9:23-24).

There is a generation that is pursuing intimacy with God as their prize, rather than praise from man. The Lord is releasing an understanding of the Zadok priesthood, which is the heart matter at this hour. Let's look at this a little closer.

King David's son, Absalom, stood at the gates of the city and convinced people that he would be a better king than his father. Zadok heard of this and brought the Ark of the Covenant to King David who was God's chosen (see 2 Sam. 15:24). Hundreds of years later, in the book of Ezekiel, we find God distributing land and inheritances. Look at what He says to the Levites who went astray:

> *""The Levites who went far from me when Israel went astray and who wandered from me after their idols must bear the consequences of their sin. They may serve in my sanctuary, having charge of the gates of the temple and serving in it; they may slaughter the burnt offerings and sacrifices for the people and stand before the people and serve them. But because they served them in the presence of their idols and made the house of Israel fall into sin, therefore I have sworn with uplifted hand that they must bear the consequences of their sin, declares the Sovereign LORD. They are not to come near to serve me as priests or come near any of my holy things or my most holy offerings; they must bear the shame of their detestable practices. Yet I will put them in charge of the duties of the temple and all the work that is to be done in it"""* (Ez. 44:10-14).

In layman's terms, the Levites who went astray would be busy ministering to people and couldn't come near to God's presence. But to the sons of Zadok the Lord says:

""But the priests, who are Levites and descendants of Zadok and who faithfully carried out the duties of my sanctuary when the Israelites went astray from me, are to come near to minister before me; they are to stand before me to offer sacrifices of fat and blood, declares the Sovereign LORD. They alone are to enter my sanctuary; they alone are to come near my table to minister before me and perform my service... They are to teach my people the difference between the holy and the common and show them how to distinguish between the unclean and the clean""" (Ez. 44:15-16, 23).

My favorite is to all who are called to be priests:

""I am to be the only inheritance the priests have. You are to give them no possession in Israel; I will be their possession""" (Ez. 44:28-29).

I don't know about you, but I would much rather have the Lord as my possession over anything this world has to offer. Paul said, *"...I consider everything a loss compared to the surpassing greatness of knowing Christ Jesus my Lord, for whose sake I have lost all things. I consider them rubbish, that I may gain Christ and be found in him..."* (Phil. 3:8). Friends, this is the longing desire of the heart of humanity: to know Christ, and be found in Him. Everything else pales in comparison, fading into the backdrop, as the Lord takes center stage in our lives. As we come to know the Lord more intimately and become acquainted with Him more personally, our hearts can't help but burn within us. This will cause us, like Paul, to declare that everything else is rubbish—there is nothing that we wouldn't lay aside to live under the smile of God. Those around us may think we're crazy, but people in love often do crazy things.

"May the grace of the Lord Jesus Christ, and the love of God, and the fellowship of the Holy Spirit be with you all" (2 Cor. 13:14).

Reflection Questions

1. What is the first purpose of the priesthood?

_____

_____

_____

_____

_____

2. According to Exodus 19:4, why did God take the children of Israel out of Egypt?

_____

_____

_____

_____

_____

3. According to John 17:3, what exactly is eternal life?

_____

_____

_____

_____

_____

4. In your own words, what is the heart of the Zadok priesthood?

_____

_____

_____

Aaron must burn fragrant incense on the altar every morning when he tends the lamps. He must burn incense again when he lights the lamps at twilight so incense will burn regularly before the LORD for the generations to come (Ex. 30:7-8).

Incense in Scripture represents the prayers of the saints.

"May my prayer be set before you like incense; may the lifting up of my hands be like the evening sacrifice" (Ps. 141:2).

Prayer simply means talking to God. Healthy communication is required in every relationship. The Lord desires to commune with us—prayer is not a monologue; it's a dialogue. Here are a few quotes that help define prayer:

"I am persuaded that God will do nothing but in answer to prayer."
    -John Wesley

"The greatest thing anyone can do for God and for man is to pray."
                                                            -S.D Gordon

"You can do more than pray after you have prayed, but you cannot do more than pray until you have prayed."
                                                            -S.D Gordon

"God shapes the world by prayer. The more praying there is in the world the better the world will be, the mightier the forces against evil... The prayers of God's saints are the capital stock of heaven by which God carries on His work upon the earth. God conditions the very life and prosperity of His cause on prayer."

-E.M Bounds

"Evangelical Christianity is lost unless it rediscovers that the source of its divine life and power is prayer."

-Frank Laubach

"The devil mocks our wisdom, laughs at our toil, but shudders when we pray."

-Dr. Tom Hignell MD

"The only power that overcomes the enemy and releases souls from his strangle–hold is the power of the Holy Spirit, and the only power that releases the power of the Holy Spirit is the power of believing prayer. "

-Bilheimer

"Through prayer we guard our chastity, control our temper and rid ourselves of vanity... Through prayer we obtain physical well-being, a happy home, and a strong, well-ordered society... Prayer is the delight of the joyful as well as the solace of the afflicted... prayer is intimacy with God and contemplation of the invisible... prayer is the enjoyment of things present and the substance of things to come."

-Gregory of Nyssa

"Prayer can do anything that God can do."

-E.M Bounds

There are many types of prayers and ways to pray as revealed in Scripture. When Jesus taught on prayer, He mostly spoke of persistent prayer. One of my favorite examples of prayer is found in the story of Elijah.

"And Elijah said to Ahab, 'Go, eat and drink, for there is the sound of a heavy rain.' So Ahab went off to eat and drink, but Elijah climbed to the top of Carmel, bent down to the ground and put his face between his knees. 'Go and look toward the sea,' he told his servant. And he went up and looked. 'There is nothing there,' he said. Seven times Elijah said, 'Go back.' The seventh time the servant reported, 'A cloud as small as a man's hand is rising from the sea'" (1 Kings 18:41-44).

James 5:17 says, *"Elijah was a man like us."* Elijah heard the word of the Lord and prayed until what God spoke to him happened. Many times people have their hopes deferred because they pray once or twice and the fulfillment of the promise doesn't happen. Elijah got into a birthing position and prayed seven times for the fulfillment of what God has promised.

I've often wondered why we have to pray for so long sometimes to get answers to our prayers. There is incredible insight about this found in the book of Daniel.

"Then he continued, 'Do not be afraid, Daniel. Since the first day that you set your mind to gain understanding and to humble yourself before your God, your words were heard, and I have come in response to them. But the prince of the Persian kingdom resisted me twenty-one days. Then Michael, one of the chief princes, came to help me, because I was detained there with the king of Persia. Now I have come to explain to you what will happen to your people in the future, for the vision concerns a time yet to come'" (Dan. 10:12-14).

God heard Daniel's prayer and answered it on the first day by sending the angel Gabriel, but the prince of Persia withheld God's promise. There can be timing to the answer of our prayers being fulfilled, but there can also be spiritual warfare. The key is to keep asking, keep seeking, and keep knocking.

"So I say to you, Ask and keep on asking and it shall be given you; seek and keep on seeking and you shall find; knock and keep on knocking and the

door shall be opened to you. For everyone who asks and keeps on asking receives; and he who seeks and keeps on seeking finds; and to him who knocks and keeps on knocking, the door shall be opened" (Luke 11:9-10 AMP).

One last story that illustrates persistent prayer is found in the book of Luke.

"Then Jesus told his disciples a parable to show them that they should always pray and not give up. He said: 'In a certain town there was a judge who neither feared God nor cared about men. And there was a widow in that town who kept coming to him with the plea, "Grant me justice against my adversary." For some time he refused. But finally he said to himself, "Even though I don't fear God or care about men, yet because this widow keeps bothering me, I will see that she gets justice, so that she won't eventually wear me out with her coming"" (Luke 18:1-5)!

Prayer is not intended to be one way. After we pray we must expect God to speak back to us. This is called listening prayer or contemplative prayer. The Bible instructs us to be still and know He is God (see Ps. 46:10). It would be rude to talk to someone for an hour and not let them speak. God wants to dialogue with us; we must position ourselves like Samuel and lie down in His presence. I like to lie down with some instrumental music playing, keeping a note pad and a pen at my side, expecting God to speak to me.

Praying to the Father in the name of Jesus

"This, then, is how you should pray: 'Our Father in heaven...'" (Matt. 6:9).

When the disciples asked Jesus how to pray, He told them to pray to the Father in His name.

"In that day you will no longer ask me anything. I tell you the truth, my Father will give you whatever you ask in my name. Until now you have not asked for anything in my name. Ask and you will receive, and your joy will be complete" (John 16:22-28).

We learn from the above scripture that when we pray to the Father in the name of Jesus, the Father will give us whatever we ask so our joy may be full. Praying in the name of Jesus means to pray in the authority and character that stands behind that name. The Bible calls us ambassadors (see 2 Cor. 5:20). An ambassador represents another nation. The ambassador of that nation has the entire authority of that nation backing him up. As we pray in Jesus' name, all of heaven backs us up.

I'll never forget one of the first times I was called upon to pray for someone in front of a crowd of people—I was so scared nothing was going to happen. I closed my eyes and in a vision I saw hands stretching forth from heaven in agreement with my prayers. All of heaven comes into agreement when we pray in the name of Jesus.

> *"Then Peter said, 'Silver or gold I do not have, but what I have I give you. In the name of Jesus Christ of Nazareth, walk.' Taking him by the right hand, he helped him up, and instantly the man's feet and ankles became strong... 'By faith in the name of Jesus, this man whom you see and know was made strong. It is Jesus' name and the faith that comes through him that has given this complete healing to him, as you can all see'"* (Acts 3:6-7, 15-16).

Intercession

Another function of the priesthood in the Old Testament was to stand in the gap and intercede on behalf of God's people. The Bible says that Jesus sat down at the right hand of the Father and intercedes for us (see Heb. 7:25). Intercession literally means to *stand in the gap.*

> *"I looked for a man among them who would build up the wall and stand before me in the gap on behalf of the land so I would not have to destroy it, but I found none"* (Ez. 22:30).

In the days of Nehemiah, the walls were broken down. This made it easy for the enemy to sneak in through a gap. While Nehemiah was repairing the walls he would station soldiers in the busted places. This, in essence, is the definition of intercession: standing in the gap so the enemy is not able to come into a person's life. Intercession is praying on another's behalf.

A great example of an intercessor is found in the story of Abraham.

> *"Then the LORD said, 'The outcry against Sodom and Gomorrah is so great and their sin so grievous that I will go down and see if what they have done is as bad as the outcry that has reached me. If not, I will know.' The men turned away and went toward Sodom, but Abraham remained standing before the LORD. Then Abraham approached him and said: 'Will you sweep away the righteous with the wicked? What if there are fifty righteous people in the city? Will you really sweep it away and not spare the place for the sake of the fifty righteous people in it? Far be it from you to do such a thing—to kill the righteous with the wicked, treating the righteous and the wicked alike. Far be it from you! Will not the Judge of all the earth do right'"* (Gen. 18:20-25)?

Abraham continues to petition the Lord according to His mercy all the way down to ten people.

> *"Then he said, 'May the Lord not be angry, but let me speak just once more. What if only ten can be found there'"* (Gen. 18:32).

Then the Lord answered, *"'...For the sake of ten, I will not destroy it.'"* Abraham had an understanding of God's mercy. He stood as a representative on the earth to plead before God for the people. Cain killed his brother Abel, and the Bible says that his blood cried out from the ground (see Heb. 12:24). His blood cried *vengeance*. Jesus Christ's blood was shed on the cross and His blood cries out for *mercy*. *"Mercy triumphs over judgment"* (James 2:13)! God's priests must learn to walk in mercy towards people. Intercessors are called to continually cry out for mercy from the Lord for those that the enemy is accusing.

The ministry of intercession is for everyone. As long as we have unsaved people in our families, or sick people on the earth, we are called to the ministry of intercession. I once heard someone say, "Intercession isn't praying *to* Jesus, but praying *with* Him." As we position ourselves to hear the Lord's voice, we will often sense or feel His heart for the situation. In turn, we take His will and pray it back to the Father.

Reflection Questions

1. What is a simple definition of prayer?

_____

_____

_____

_____

_____

2. Can you list a few different styles / types of prayer?

_____

_____

_____

_____

_____

3. Why is prayer so important?

_____

_____

_____

_____

_____

4. What does it mean to pray in the name of Jesus?

_____

_____

_____

_____

_____

5. What is the definition of intercession described in this chapter? Who is called to intercession?

_____

_____

_____

_____

6. What are some things that hinder or have hindered your prayer life? What are some practical things you can implement daily to bump up and strengthen your prayer life?

_____

_____

_____

_____

_____

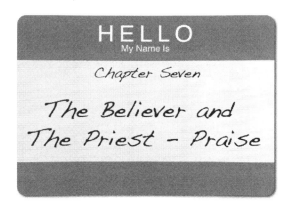

But You are holy, Enthroned in the praises of Israel
(Ps. 22:3 NKJV).

Praise is part of the ministry of the priests—it accomplishes many things. The word *enthroned* in this passage is the Hebrew word *yashab*, which means to *dwell, settle, and remain*. God dwells in the atmosphere of His praise—He really does inhabit the praises of His people. Praise creates a place for God to dwell, settle down, and remain.

"Enter his gates with thanksgiving and his courts with praise..." (Ps. 100:4).

Praise not only creates a place for Him to dwell, but provides a way for us to enter into His presence. Praise brings us into the awesomeness of His glory. The more we fix our eyes on Jesus in worship and praise, the more we are transformed into His image and likeness. We are a royal priesthood who gives praise to a holy and worthy King.

"But you are a chosen people, a royal priesthood, a holy nation, a people belonging to God, that you may declare the praises of him who called you out of darkness into his wonderful light" (1 Peter 2:9).

Take a moment to read over and meditate on the seven Hebrew words for *praise* found in the box on the following page.

Here are seven Hebrew words for *praise*:

Halall
-To shine, to rave
-To praise, to boast
-To be clamorously foolish
-To act madly

Yadah
-To revere or worship, to give thanks or praise (with extended hands)
-To lift the hands

Barak
-To bless, to kneel, to salute

Tehilla
-A song or a hymn of praise
-Spontaneous expression of spiritual song

Zamar
-To make music, to sing praise
-To play a musical instrument
-To pluck and twang

Towdah
-Thanksgiving, praise, confession

Shabach
-To exclaim, to shout
-To laud, praise, commend

(A study taken from Selah Ministries—Ray Hughes)

As we can see by these seven Hebrew words for *praise*, praise requires action. Praise is exuberant and expressive, praising God with our entire being.

"David, wearing a linen ephod, danced before the LORD with all his might, while he and the entire house of Israel brought up the ark of the LORD with shouts and the sound of trumpets.... When David returned home to bless his household, Michal daughter of Saul came out to meet him and said, 'How the

king of Israel has distinguished himself today, disrobing in the sight of the slave girls and his servants as any vulgar fellow would!' David said to Michal, 'It was before the LORD, who chose me rather than your father or anyone from his house when he appointed me ruler over the LORD'S people Israel—I will celebrate before the LORD. I will become even more undignified than this, and I will be humiliated in my own eyes...'" (2 Sam. 6:14-15, 20-22).

David danced radically before his God. When Michal commented of David's behavior, David proclaimed He would have become even more undignified! For a King to wear his linen ephod in front of people would be humiliating. But David was willing to do anything to humble himself before his King.

Battling with Praise

"The Israelites went up to Bethel and inquired of God. They said, 'Who of us shall go first to fight against the Benjamites?' The LORD replied, 'Judah shall go first'" (Judg. 20:18).

The Lord sent the tribe of Judah into battle first. The word *Judah* means *praise*. From this story, we learn that when we're going into battle, Judah should come first—praise clears the way and disarms enemy attacks. We find the same lesson in 2 Chronicles 20:20-25. The Lord gave Jehoshaphat a strategy for defeating the enemy armies: the worship team goes in first. In both of these stories God's people were victorious in battle. It's easy to praise God after the battle is won, but praising God while facing the battle isn't always easy.

However, we should also praise Him when we aren't facing battle at all. Early in my walk with God I had a vision of an airplane flying. Suddenly the airplane began to lose altitude as if it were going to crash. I heard the shouts and cries of the passengers asking Jesus to save them. In the spirit I saw a hand come under the airplane and steady it—the shouts and cries stopped. The Lord spoke to my heart and said these were people who only came to Him in crisis. His mercy would be there for them, but who would praise Him when there is no crisis?

We see why we praise Him in 1 Peter 2:9—"...*that you may declare the praises of him who called you out of darkness into his wonderful light."* When we consider life without Jesus, we realize it is by grace, and grace alone, that we are saved. It is important to remember how great a salvation we have been given.

Praise Brings Deliverance

"About midnight Paul and Silas were praying and singing hymns to God, and the other prisoners were listening to them. Suddenly there was such a violent earthquake that the foundations of the prison were shaken. At once all the prison doors flew open, and everybody's chains came loose" (Acts 16:25-26).

As Paul and Silas were in prison, they prayed and sang hymns to God. In the Greek, singing hymns means to sing praises. Paul and Silas were praising God in prison and God set them free.

There are many people in the body of Christ that struggle with depression. We are instructed to put on the *garment of praise* for the *spirit of heaviness* (see Isa. 61:3 NKJV). As we lift our voices in worship and high praise, telling Him how great and awesome He is, we begin to take our eyes off ourselves and our current condition and put them on Jesus. Our perspective changes from looking at our inability to His ability. We are not an army that marches towards the enemy. We are an army that marches towards the face of God seeking intimacy through worship and praise.

The Bible says the horse is prepared for the day of battle but victory belongs to the Lord (see Prov. 21:31). The mental picture here is a boxer training for a big fight. He steps into the ring with the devil ready to fight. As soon as the bell rings, before he gets to throw a punch, God knocks the devil out. The victory belongs to the Lord.

I have met people that always seem to be under attack. This has more to do with their perspective than actually being attacked by the devil. It is true that the enemy sends attacks our way, but *"If God is for us, who can be against us"* (Rom. 8:31)? If I were standing at the foot of a large mountain, it would seem overwhelming. But if I were to look at the same mountain from heaven, it wouldn't seem overwhelming at all. As we worship God, the things that seem impossible become possible. Let us, as God's priests, fight using one of our greatest weapons: fixing our eyes on Jesus and giving Him praise.

While I was in India I had an encounter I will never forget. I felt the Lord draw me away to pray. As I was praying, I could hear a man chanting close by. I felt like the man was speaking curses against the crusade that was being held. I asked the Lord what to do. The Lord spoke to me out of Psalms 149:6-9—*"May the praise of God be in their mouths and a double-edged sword in their hands, to inflict vengeance on the nations and punishment on the peoples, to bind their kings with fetters, their nobles with shackles of iron, to carry out the sentence written against them. This is the glory of all his saints. Praise the LORD."* Scripture declares that we don't wrestle with flesh or blood (see Eph. 6:12). Our war is not against people but demonic spiritual forces. This scripture is saying our high praise is like a sword—a weapon of battle—binding demonic spirits. Spiritual warfare is not intended to be exclusively focused on the devil, but as we lift our voices to God, He destroys our enemies. When the Lord showed me this scripture I began to praise Him out loud and sing in the Spirit. As I did this, the man's chanting stopped. I realized that as I praised God, the demon that was influencing the man was bound. Wow! That's the kind of fighting I want to do. The battle is truly the Lord's.

Reflection Questions

1. What is one way we can enter into God's presence?

_____

_____

_____

_____

2. What exactly is praise? Why is praise so important?

_____

_____

_____

_____

3. What does praise do to the enemy?

_____

_____

_____

_____

_____

Worship today, for many people, means to sing slow songs to Jesus. Worship can take the form of singing slow songs to the Lord, but biblically the definition and theme of worship greatly exceeds mere singing.

In studying the Bible, there is a term called the *law of first mention*. The law of first mention is when we go back to the first occurrence of a specific topic mentioned in the Bible, and thoroughly study the topic in order gain understanding and meaning of it from that particular passage.

Taking the law of first mention into consideration, let's look at the first passage in Scripture where we find the word *worship*.

> *"He said to his servants, 'Stay here with the donkey while I and the boy go over there. We will worship and then we will come back to you"* (Gen. 22:5).

This verse is taken from one of the many Old Testament stories about Abraham. Abraham is preparing to sacrifice his son Isaac on the altar because the Lord had asked him to. The heart behind true worship is sacrifice. This remains the same in the New Testament. As we live our lives fully submitted to God, it is a spiritual act of worship.

> *"Therefore, I urge you, brothers, in view of God's mercy, to offer your bodies as living sacrifices, holy and pleasing to God—this is your spiritual act of worship. Do not conform any longer to the pattern of this world, but be transformed by the renewing of your mind. Then you will be able to test and*

approve what God's will is—his good, pleasing and perfect will" (Rom. 12:1-2).

What then do we do with the passage where Jesus says He desires mercy and not sacrifice? Let's look at it closer to understand the context:

"While Jesus was having dinner at Matthew's house, many tax collectors and 'sinners' came and ate with him and his disciples. When the Pharisees saw this, they asked his disciples, 'Why does your teacher eat with tax collectors and 'sinners'? On hearing this, Jesus said, 'It is not the healthy who need a doctor, but the sick. But go and learn what this means: "I desire mercy, not sacrifice." For I have not come to call the righteous, but sinners'" (Matt. 9:10-13).

Jesus was quoting an Old Testament passage, Hosea 6:6—*"For I desire mercy and not sacrifice...."* The Pharisees were more concerned with keeping to the letter of the law and outward signs of righteousness, than knowing God. Continually in Jesus' ministry we find Him breaking Jewish laws and customs. One example is when Jesus prayed for a person and healed them on the Sabbath. The Pharisees were abiding by the Law of Moses which was given by God and was truth. However, Jesus was showing a higher truth: *love and mercy*. So it remains, submitting ourselves to God is sacrifice and is a spiritual act of worship.

The Old Testament Hebrew word for worship is *shachah*, which means, *to worship, prostrate oneself, bow down.* The New Testament Greek word for worship is *proskuneo* which has a similar meaning: *to make obeisance, do reverence to, kiss.* We can sing songs of adoration to God as a sign of worship, but our lifestyle is meant to be an act of worship to God. As we obey God in our lives and humble ourselves, we bow down and kiss His feet. Worship is not an event but a lifestyle.

"'Sir,' the woman said, 'I can see that you are a prophet. Our fathers worshiped on this mountain, but you Jews claim that the place where we must worship is in Jerusalem.' Jesus declared, 'Believe me, woman, a time is coming when you will worship the Father neither on this mountain nor in

Jerusalem. You Samaritans worship what you do not know; we worship what we do know, for salvation is from the Jews. Yet a time is coming and has now come when the true worshipers will worship the Father in spirit and truth, for they are the kind of worshipers the Father seeks. God is spirit, and his worshipers must worship in spirit and truth'" (John 4:19-24).

The Samaritans believed that worship could only take place on one specific mountain. But Jesus crushed that idea by saying you don't have to be on a mountain or in Jerusalem; God is simply looking for someone to worship Him in spirit and in truth. It is, however, important to come together as the body of Christ to worship and fellowship, but we don't need to wait for the Sunday worship service to do this. Worshiping God is a lifestyle. Worshiping the Father in spirit and truth means worshipping Him with our everything—our entire heart exposed—nothing hidden. We can all do this anywhere and at anytime.

"Speak to one another with psalms, hymns and spiritual songs. Sing and make music in your heart to the Lord, always giving thanks to God the Father for everything, in the name of our Lord Jesus Christ" (Eph. 5:19-20).

We can sing and make music in our hearts continually. Noah, Adam, and Enoch, to mention of few, walked with God. We are called to walk with God in continual communion. How is this possible in such a busy society?

"But when you pray, go into your room, close the door and pray to your Father, who is unseen" (Matt. 6:6).

Secret places have secret entrances. It's necessary to find quiet time, free from the distractions of the world, to be with God. But it's also equally important to learn to cultivate a lifestyle of prayer and worship while living in the world and doing day to day activities. I've learned to cherish every moment alone: while in the shower, brushing my teeth, driving my car, and on my bed when I get up in the morning and lay down at night. These are times when I find a place of stillness and peace in my heart to praise God and give Him thanks. When we continually worship Him, we are cultivating His very presence in our lives.

There is a man in the Old Testament named Obed-Edom who had the pleasure of having the Ark of the Covenant in his house for three months. King David was carrying the Ark of the Covenant on an oxcart. When the oxen stumbled, a man named Uzzah reached out to steady the Ark to keep it from falling. When he touched it he fell down dead. David wasn't sure what he should do, so he decided to take the Ark of the Covenant into Obed-Edom's house.

> *"The ark of the LORD remained in the house of Obed-Edom the Gittite for three months, and the LORD blessed him and his entire household"* (2 Sam. 6:11).

The Ark of the Covenant is where the presence of God dwelt in the Old Testament. One of the greatest desires of my heart is that God Himself would move into my home. What's even more amazing is the home He wants to dwell in is me! Worshiping God creates a place in our hearts and lives for Him to rest and abide—He makes His home with us.

> *"'However, the Most High does not live in houses made by men. As the prophet says: "Heaven is my throne, and the earth is my footstool. What kind of house will you build for me?" says the Lord. "Or where will my resting place be"'"* (Acts 7:48-49)?

One evening in a dream I saw a man who I recognize as an anointed teacher. He spoke to me and said, "I see an angel standing next to you and he's touching your temple." Then he said, "House of prayer." He then laid his hands on me. I woke up, and in the natural, felt the power of God. As I pondered the dream, understanding came to me. The Lord, as a teacher, was teaching me that my temple is a house of prayer. There are places you can go and pray, but the Lord desires that you, being the temple of the Holy Spirit, become a place of continual prayer, praise, and worship.

Reflection Questions

1. According to the law of first mention, what is the heart behind worship?

_____

_____

_____

_____

2. What is the biblical definition of worship?

_____

_____

_____

_____

3. Where is your secret place with God?

_____

_____

_____

_____

_____

4. Take a moment and ask the Holy Spirit for some ways you could further cultivate a lifestyle of prayer, praise, and worship.

_____

_____

_____

_____

_____

- NOTES -

HELLO
My Name Is

Chapter Nine

The Believer and The Priest – Power

When Jesus had called the Twelve together, he gave them power and
authority to drive out all demons and to cure diseases, and he sent them out
to preach the kingdom of God and to heal the sick (Luke 9:1-2).

The power of God is given to the priests of God and is the result of prayer and time with the Lord. The Bible says, *"They were perceived to be uneducated and unlearned men but they had been with Jesus"* (Acts 4:13). As we spend time with Jesus, the anointing on Him rubs off onto us. The word *anoint* means to *rub or smear*. Acts 10:38 says, *"...God anointed Jesus of Nazareth with the Holy Spirit and power, and how he went around doing good and healing all who were under the power of the devil, because God was with him."* This scripture is saying that God rubbed and smeared the Holy Spirit and power all over Jesus. As we spend time with the Lord in prayer, the Holy Spirit begins to rest on us releasing His power.

One of the Greek words translated as power in the New Testament is the word *dunamis*. Dunamis is the miracle working power of God—the supernatural strength and ability from heaven that is released upon earth to make the impossible possible. The English word *dynamite* originated from the Greek word dunamis. Dunamis is the explosive, dynamite, miracle working power of God.

Take a moment to look over and meditate on the points and Scripture references found in the box on the following page concerning Dunamis Power.

Listed below are a few key points that should help you receive a more complete understanding of *Dunamis Power*.

* We are clothed with *Dunamis Power* to witness about Jesus (see Acts 1:8).

* The Kingdom of God is not in word but *Dunamis Power* (see 1 Cor. 4:20).

* We are called to go forth in the spirit and *Dunamis Power* of Elijah, to turn the hearts of the children to the fathers, the hearts of the fathers to the children, to bring justice, to turn the disobedient to the wisdom of the righteousness, and to make ready and prepare a people for the Lord (see Luke 1:17).

* Jesus returned in the *Dunamis Power* of the Spirit after His time of being tempted in the desert (see Luke 4:14).

* Stephen was filled with grace and *Dunamis Power* and did great wonders and miraculous signs among people (see Acts 6:8).

* The message of the cross is *Dunamis Power* (see 1 Cor. 1:18).

* There is *Dunamis Power* released into our lives through the resurrection of Jesus (see Phil. 3:10).

* Christ is the *Dunamis Power* of God (see 1 Cor. 1:24).

* The enemy has his own counterfeit *Dunamis Power* (see 2 Thess. 2:9 and Luke 10:19). However, we have authority over his power (see Luke 10:19).

The dunamis power of God is associated with being a witness:

> *"But you will receive power when the Holy Spirit comes on you; and you will be my witnesses in Jerusalem, and in all Judea and Samaria, and to the ends of the earth"* (Acts. 1:8).

Found in Acts 1:8 is a huge key to releasing people into the harvest. If I were to testify in court to what someone told me happened, that would be called hearsay or rumor. A witness is someone who has seen with his own eyes. There are many valid ways to share God's love with people; the easiest to me is to sharing what I've seen.

Let's say you're at work getting a cup of coffee. One of your coworkers asks you how your weekend was. You respond, "I had an amazing weekend at church on Sunday, a woman who was born completely deaf was healed." Can you imagine the response that person would have? This is why it's critical to continually press in to see God's power in Church. People can then simply share what they've seen with their own eyes. As priests of the Most High, we are called to take the power of God we receive through prayer to those in need around us.

> *"All this is from God, who reconciled us to himself through Christ and gave us the ministry of reconciliation: that God was reconciling the world to himself in Christ, not counting men's sins against them. And he has committed to us the message of reconciliation. We are therefore Christ's ambassadors, as though God were making his appeal through us. We implore you on Christ's behalf: Be reconciled to God. God made him who had no sin to be sin for us, so that in him we might become the righteousness of God"* (2 Cor. 5:18-21).

We have been given the ministry of reconciliation as believers. The word *reconcile* means *to make friends with again.* We are called to introduce people to the One who loves us to wholeness with gentleness. We have a good message to give the world: God is not angry with you; He is Love, and desires for you to get to know Him and spend lots of time together—eternity. However, when our message of God's love is united with His power, we will see much greater effectiveness.

Signs, Wonders, and Miracles

Multitudes came to Jesus to be healed and then to hear the word of God. I have witnessed this with my own eyes. In my travels overseas I have seen people wait for hours in the rain to get prayer for healing because they heard that Jesus is healing people. They first witness and experience God's power; then listen to a message of love and acceptance, giving their entire lives to Him. Signs and wonders demonstrate to the multitudes that God is real, and He loves them.

"As you go, preach this message: 'The kingdom of heaven is near.' Heal the sick, raise the dead, cleanse those who have leprosy, drive out demons. Freely you have received, freely give" (Matt. 10:7-8).

Jesus' ministry was filled with numerous accounts of people being healed and set free. Jesus ascended into heaven and sent us His Holy Spirit to enable us to continue the ministry that He modeled for us while on the earth. Signs, wonders, and miracles are part of the gospel. The apostle Paul goes as far as saying that we are not fully preaching the gospel if there are not signs and wonders.

"...by the power of signs and miracles, through the power of the Spirit. So from Jerusalem all the way around to Illyricum, I have fully proclaimed the gospel of Christ" (Rom. 15:19).

John the Baptist asked his disciples to go find Jesus and ask Him if He was the Messiah or if there was another. Jesus responded in Matthew 11:4-5 and said, *"'Go back and report to John what you hear and see: The blind receive sight, the lame walk, those who have leprosy are cured, the deaf hear, the dead are raised, and the good news is preached to the poor.'"* Signs and wonders follow the preaching of the gospel. According to Mark 16:16-18 the ministry of praying for the sick is not intended only for those who have gifts of healing: *"Whoever believes and is baptized will be saved, but whoever does not believe will be condemned. And these signs will accompany those who believe: In my name they will drive out demons; they will speak in new tongues; they will pick up snakes with their hands; and when they drink deadly poison, it will not hurt them at all; they will place their hands on sick people, and they will get well."* If you are a born again believer, these signs should accompany you: casting out demons, speaking in tongues, destroying the work of the enemy, and seeing the sick get well.

Once when I was a young Christian, I was part of a very large crusade in Quito, Ecuador, in South America. A man came up to me for prayer. I asked what was wrong with him and he pointed to a very large tumor on his head. I thought to myself, "Oh no, God, couldn't you have let me pray for someone with a bad back?" I was worried that when I prayed nothing would happen and everyone would see because we were on a platform. I closed my eyes and prayed something like, "Oh God, I just want to go home, what I am I doing here? Please help!" When I looked up at the man the tumor was gone and he was completely healed. God healed the man despite my lack of faith! All we have to do is stretch forth our hands and He does the rest.

I have often stumbled into God's will. Once while I was part of a ministry team Mexico, I was hanging out with some friends before the evening crusade. We were standing outside a store and the woman inside asked us if we wanted to purchase any wine. Being silly I said, "I don't need that wine, I have the new wine; have you ever heard of it?" I wasn't trying to be evangelistic. She said, "No, I haven't." I thought that I better tell her about the Holy Spirit now. I told her about how after Jesus ascended into heaven the Holy Spirit came to live inside of us. She said that she was a Catholic but had never heard about this. I asked if she wanted to receive the Holy Spirit; she said "Yes." I led her in a prayer of repentance and asked Jesus to fill her with His Spirit. I asked her if she wanted prayer for anything else and she informed us of three cysts in her breasts. After my friends and I prayed, she went to the bathroom to check if she was healed. She came out and said two of the three cysts were completely gone. One of the names of God not found in Scripture is *Jehovah Sneaky*. We will often find ourselves in positions that we wouldn't get ourselves into—but He knows. Christianity is fun.

Evangelism can start off as an outreach, but should end up becoming part of everyday life. We are called to walk in the power of God and release it everywhere we go—this is called being supernaturally natural.

Reflection Questions

1. What is one of the keys to releasing people into the harvest?

_____

_____

_____

_____

2. Have you ever witnessed a miracle? Share in a group setting what you saw and what the fruit was?

_____

_____

_____

_____

3. Why did the multitudes come to Jesus?

_____

_____

_____

_____

4. Write out John 10:37 and meditate on it.

_____

_____

_____

_____

God gave the keys to the kingdom to Adam; Adam sinned and gave the keys of the kingdom to Satan. Jesus came to the earth as the last Adam and died on the cross becoming the last sacrifice. Jesus made a public spectacle of principalities and powers, destroying the power of death and sin on the cross. Jesus took back the keys of the kingdom and gave them to the church.

> *"I will give you the keys of the kingdom of heaven; and whatever you bind (declare to be improper and unlawful) on earth must be what is already bound in heaven; and whatever you loose (declare lawful) on earth must be what is already loosed in heaven"* (Matt. 16:19 AMP).

The keys of the kingdom represent authority. Authority is given to God's people to determine what is, or is not, permitted to happen on the earth. God's first commission to man was to be fruitful, multiply, subdue the earth, and have dominion (see Gen. 1:28). That is still the commission today. Jesus told us to pray for God's kingdom to come and be manifested on earth as it is in heaven. The word *kingdom* means *the king's domain*. The kingdom is the rule and reign of King Jesus that is released through the Holy Spirit that dwells within us. We belong to a kingdom that is not of this world, and are called to release it upon the earth.

There is an awesome transition taking place in the church today. The Lord is releasing a greater understanding of the gospel of the kingdom. The gospel of salvation is extremely important, but it is only part of the gospel of the kingdom that Jesus preached. After we receive Christ and are born again, our life in the Spirit has just begun. We enter into a kingdom where our Father is the King. The gospel of the kingdom releases people to do what they are called to do, in all aspects of life. In times past, those who are called to be incredible mothers and fathers have felt lower, even insignificant, compared to the person standing in the pulpit. This can't be further from the truth! God loves all people the same. Success in Christ has nothing to do with what you do or how much you get paid for doing it, but walking in obedience to what the Lord has personally asked you to do. That is where the understanding of the body of Christ becomes so important.

> *"Now the body is not made up of one part but of many. If the foot should say, 'Because I am not a hand, I do not belong to the body,' it would not for that reason cease to be part of the body. And if the ear should say, 'Because I am not an eye, I do not belong to the body,' it would not for that reason cease to be part of the body. If the whole body were an eye, where would the sense of hearing be? If the whole body were an ear, where would the sense of smell be? But in fact God has arranged the parts in the body, every one of them, just as he wanted them to be. If they were all one part, where would the body be? As it is, there are many parts, but one body"* (1 Cor. 12:14-20).

In today's society, the man or woman on stage receives more credit than the person who is responsible for cleaning the building. The truth of the matter is the meeting couldn't take place without the person responsible for cleaning, setting up chairs, and doing sound. All of those roles help the meeting flow so God's people can better experience His presence. In 1975, Bill Bright, founder of *Campus Crusade*, and Loren Cunningham, founder of *Youth With A Mission*, had lunch together. God simultaneously gave each of them a message to give to the other: "The culture is shaped by seven mind-molders or mountains in society. If we can influence each of these areas for Christ, we will win the culture of our nation." The seven mountains are:

1) *Arts and Entertainment*
2) *Business*
3) *Education*
4) *Family*
5) *Government*
6) *Religion*
7) *Media*

The Lord is raising people up to infiltrate each of these spheres of influence. In times past, many of these areas were considered *unclean* by the church. In the Old Testament if someone touched a person with leprosy, they would be considered unclean. In the New Testament, however, those who Jesus touched became clean. The Lord wants to redeem those things which we have, in the past, considered ungodly. To date, the movie *Passion of the Christ* has been viewed by more people than any other movie in history. The Lord has used that movie to enter into the households of people who have secretly been curious about the gospel, but would never step foot into a church building. It's a new day.

We are called to advance into enemy territory and take ground for the kingdom of God. We can do this at any job, any school, and any place. The jobs we have now should be considered the sphere of influence that God has chosen for us to impact. If you're called to ministry it doesn't necessarily mean you should work in a church. I've met so many people waiting to step into fulltime ministry while they are miserable at their workplace. We need a radical mindset shift, and God is doing it. The Holy Spirit in this hour is releasing a revelation of Christ in you, the hope of glory.

The bride of Christ must begin to see herself the way God sees her. There is a very familiar story in the book of Numbers where God sends His people to spy out the Promised Land. They see giants and get scared. *"We saw the Nephilim there. We seemed like grasshoppers in our own eyes, and we looked the same to them"* (Num. 13:32-33). The book of Proverbs says it another way, *"For as he thinks in his heart, so is he"* (Prov. 23:7 NKJV). If we are going to step into our God-given potential, it's necessary to see ourselves the way God sees us. Many people I meet ask me, "Isn't moving in the power of God and getting prophetic revelation only for the superstars?" This couldn't be further from the truth. The Lord, from the beginning of the Bible to the end, uses men and women that we would probably overlook. Moses had a problem with his speech, Gideon complains he was from the weakest tribe, John the Baptist wore camel's hair and munched on wild locusts and honey. None of these people would probably be our first pick. Our God doesn't call those who are qualified; He qualifies those who are called. If God calls you king, you are king.

"...and have redeemed us to God by Your blood out of every tribe and tongue and people and nation, and have made us kings and priests to our God; and we shall reign on the earth" (Rev. 5:9-10 NKJV).

Because we have been redeemed by the blood of Jesus Christ, we have been set apart for the plans and purposes of God. We have been made kings, called to rule and reign with Christ, establishing His heavenly kingdom on earth.

"But seek first the kingdom of God and His righteousness, and all these things shall be added to you" (Matt. 6:33 NKJV).

When we make the kingdom of God our primary concern, God will provide everything we need. Kings have great riches, and because we are kings we should not be in lack. *"Beloved, I pray that you may prosper in all things and be in health, just as your soul prospers"* (3 John 1:2). We should prosper in every area of our lives, being fruitful and taking dominion over the realm of earth with the kingdom of heaven. Kings take care of the people in their kingdom—God wants to bless us so we can bless others. The kingly anointing often attracts financial provision, so we can, in turn, be generous to others: *"You will be made rich in every way so that you can be generous on every occasion, and through us your generosity will result in thanksgiving to God"* (2 Cor. 9:11).

Kings carry the highest level of authority in the land—authority that no other person carries. In the next section, *The Authority of the Believer,* you will learn about the authority you possess as a child of God, how to exercise your authority as a king, and ways to advance the kingdom of heaven on earth.

Reflection Questions

1. Who has the keys to the kingdom right now?

_____

_____

_____

_____

_____

2. What do the keys represent?

_____

_____

_____

_____

_____

3. What are the seven mountains of influence described in this chapter?

_____

_____

_____

_____

_____

4. To which mountain(s) do you feel called? Explain below.

_____

_____

_____

_____

- NOTES -

Part 3
Authority of the Believer

When Jesus had called the Twelve together, he gave them POWER and AUTHORITY to drive out all demons and to cure diseases, and he sent them out to preach the kingdom of God and to heal the sick
(Luke 9:1-2, emphasis mine).

As children of God, we have been given power and authority to see the miraculous manifest in our midst. In chapter nine we discussed the topic of *Dunamis,* the Greek word meaning *explosive, miracle working power.* As we learned earlier, we have the ability as born-again believers to access and release Dunamis power. In this section, *The Authority of the Believer*, we will not only talk about the *power* we carry as Christians, but the *authority* as well.

The Greek word for *authority* is *Exousia. Exousia* means *delegated authority, right, jurisdiction, freedom, force, capacity, power, and strength.* As you see in the above scripture, Jesus gave His twelve followers both power and authority (Dunamis and Exousia). Both of these are different, yet they work together. A police officer is a great example of authority. If you are driving and you look in your rear-view mirror and see those flashing lights, you pull over. Why? The entire United States government stands behind those lights. The police officer has jurisdiction to pull you over. As ambassadors for the kingdom of heaven, we have authority in our spoken words, prayers, and in Jesus' name— what we say goes, goes.

A good example of power would be that same police officer using his gun—he's using power or force. He would also be using his power to write somebody a ticket or arrest them.

An average person has the power or ability to use a gun, handcuff somebody, or write a ticket on a piece of paper, but only a police officer has the authority to do all that stuff. We have both power, and the authority to exercise it.

The authority that we have is not found in anything that we've done or can do. It's not something we strive to acquire or to earn. The authority that we posses as children of God is found in the finished work of the cross, the resurrection, in the name of Jesus, and Christ in you the hope of glory. Our authority comes from the person of Jesus Christ.

> *"Then Jesus came to them and said, 'All authority in heaven and on earth has been given to me. Therefore go and make disciples of all nations, baptizing them in the name of the Father and of the Son and of the Holy Spirit, and teaching them to obey everything I have commanded you. And surely I am with you always, to the very end of the age'"* (Matt. 28:17-20).

In the verse above, Jesus is commissioning His followers one last time before He goes into heaven. He's commanding us to make disciples of all nations, baptizing them, and teaching them to walk according to His teachings. When heaven received Him, He sat down at the Father's right hand, showing us His earthly ministry was complete; He came and finished what He was supposed to do. Since He finished what He had to do, we pick up where He left off. Take a look at the commission Mark records before Jesus is taken up into heaven:

> *"He said to them, 'Go into all the world and preach the good news to all creation. Whoever believes and is baptized will be saved, but whoever does not believe will be condemned. And these signs will accompany those who believe: in my name they will drive out demons; they will speak in new tongues; they will pick up snakes with their hands; and when they drink deadly poison, it will not hurt them at all; they will place their hands on sick people, and they will get well'"* (Mark 16:15-18).

This verse states that if we believe, we have authority in Jesus' name to cast out demons, speak in tongues, pick up snakes, drink deadly poison without being harmed, and heal the sick. These are signs that cause people to wonder—they follow us as we preach the gospel of the kingdom. Look at the next two verses:

"After the Lord Jesus had spoken to them, he was taken up into heaven and he sat at the right hand of God. Then the disciples went out and preached everywhere, and the Lord worked with them and confirmed his word by the signs that accompanied it" (Mark 16:19-20).

As you can see, Jesus finished His earthly ministry by taking a seat at the right hand of God. However, He goes on to work with His disciples by displaying signs following their preaching. True authority flows from walking in relationship with Jesus.

Authority in our Spoken Words

The avenue in which we exercise our God-given authority is through the spoken word. Jesus said, *"The words I have spoken to you are spirit and they are life..."* (John 6:63). What we speak out of our mouths aren't just words we hear for a second and then cease to exist. Words leave our mouths, rippling out into space and time, until they accomplish their purpose. The words Jesus spoke to His disciples were made of a spiritual substance that carried and imparted life. Likewise, our words are made of a spiritual substance, and we have the power to speak good things or bad things—life or death. Proverbs 18:21 says, *"Death and life are in the power of the tongue..."* (NKJV). James and Paul both exhort us to bless only, and not to curse (see James 3:9-12; Rom. 12:14); they had a deep understanding of the power and authority contained in the spoken word. Paul goes as far as to say, *"Do not let any unwholesome talk come out of your mouths, but only what is helpful for building others up according to their needs, that it may benefit those who listen"* (Eph. 4:29).

Let's observe the story of centurion and learn from his understanding of authority:

"When Jesus had entered Capernaum, a centurion came to him, asking for help. 'Lord,' he said, 'my servant lies at home paralyzed and in terrible suffering.' Jesus said to him, 'I will go and heal him.' The centurion replied, 'Lord, I do not deserve to have you come under my roof. But just say the word, and my servant will be healed. For I myself am a man under

authority, with soldiers under me. I tell this one, "Go," and he goes; and that one, "Come," and he comes. I say to my servant, "Do this," and he does it.' When Jesus heard this, he was astonished and said to those following him, 'I tell you the truth, I have not found anyone in Israel with such great faith'" (Matt. 8:5-11).

Jesus was astonished by this man's great faith. The centurion servant was a man under authority; he understood that when somebody gives a command, it happens. The man knew that no matter where Jesus was, He simply had to speak the word and his servant would be healed. Jesus has given us this same authority to bind and to loose things in the spiritual realm. He's given us keys to open and shut doors in heavenly places.

"I will give you the keys of the kingdom of heaven; whatever you bind on earth will be bound in heaven, and whatever you loose on earth will be loosed in heaven'" (Matt. 16:19).

Keys to Walking in Power and Authority

Below are some keys that will help loose God's power in your life, and enable you to walk in your authority as a believer.

 Time with Jesus

Because all genuine power and authority flows from Jesus, spending time in His presence is the primary way for His anointing to rub off on us. Not to mention, when we spend time with Him, we are led by Him, so He can show us how to unlock true power. We also find our identities in Him, causing us to understand the authority we posses.

"Now when they saw the boldness of Peter and John, and perceived that they were uneducated and untrained men, they marveled. And they realized that they had been with Jesus" (Acts 4:13 NKJV).

Purity

Jesus said that the pure in heart will see God (see Matthew 5:8). Sin corrodes our lives   in numerous ways. It's important to pursue godliness and righteousness.   Jesus prayed to His Father that we wouldn't be taken out of the world, but that we would   be   kept   from evil. We can't change the world unless we're in it, and truly   love the people who are in it—however, it's important for us to flee from ungodliness. As Paul encouraged Timothy, I also encourage you, *"But you, man   of God, flee from all this, and pursue righteousness, godliness, faith, love, endurance and gentleness."* (II Timothy 6:11).

> *"But know that the LORD has set apart for Himself him who is godly..."* (Ps. 4:3 NKJV).

 Prayer

As we learned in Chapter Six, *The Believer and the Priest—Prayer*, there are many different types of prayer. All of them are beneficial for releasing the kingdom of heaven into the realm of earth. Prayer is simply communication with God; it's the door that offers us access to the supernatural realm and all of heaven's provision.

> *"After they prayed, the place where they were meeting was shaken. And they were all filled with the Holy Spirit and spoke the word of God boldly"* (Acts 4:31).

 Fasting

Fasting is often overlooked by many Christians. For those who don't have a grid for the spiritual, fasting makes no sense and is shrugged off as useless. But in reality, fasting is a vital key that plugs us directly into the realm of the supernatural—bringing us into alignment with the kingdom of God and sharpening our spiritual senses by leaps and bounds. Fasting is actually a practice that   positions us in a place of dependence upon God—it's a place of humility which allows the grace us God to abound in our lives (see

James 4:6). Sometimes fasting is the only way for a particular anointing to be imparted into our lives, giving us supernatural ability or breakthrough. We see this when Jesus' disciples were unable to cast a demon out of a child.

"However, this kind does not go out except by prayer and fasting" (Matt. 17:21).

 Word of God

The Bible holds many promises to us from God. When we know the Word of God we know His promises, His plans, and His desires for us, His children. We can then speak His Word over our lives and the lives of others—seeing His promises come to pass. The Word of God brings clarity and focus in our lives, helping us find security in the provision of Christ. When the enemy tries to harass and deceive us, the Word of God is our anchor that keeps us from drifting away. When ministering in the prophetic, often times the Word of God that is in me, from hours of reading and studying, is quickened, giving me the ability to accurately deliver an encouraging word to an individual.

"Let the word of Christ dwell in you richly as you teach and admonish one another..." (Col. 3:16).

 Faith

Faith rests in Christ's ability, not in our own. Faith is not contrived or worked up or founded on our capability to do something. Genuine faith is complete trust and full dependence on His faithfulness. Faith reaches into the realm of the unseen and tugs on the promise until it manifests in the natural. We can, however, cultivate and mature our faith by integrating all of the keys listed above into our daily lives. Faith grows as we come to experience God's faithfulness in our lives, witness the miraculous in our midst, and see a manifestation of His promises. Faith is trusting God—it's an issue of the heart. Faith makes the impossible possible—just believe.

"'I tell you the truth, if you have faith as small as a mustard seed, you can say to this mountain, "Move from here to there" and it will move. Nothing will be impossible for you'" (Matt. 17:20).

Reflection Questions

1. What does the word *authority* mean?

_____

_____

_____

_____

2. Explain the difference between *power* and authority. Please give examples.

_____

_____

_____

_____

3. How do we release the authority we've been given by God?

_____

_____

_____

_____

4. What keys talked about in this chapter could you incorporate into your life to see a greater manifestation of God's glory?

_____

_____

_____

_____

- NOTES -

HELLO
My Name Is

Chapter Twelve

Authority Over Sin and The Devil

...because through Christ Jesus the law of the Spirit of life set me free from the law of sin and death (Rom. 8:2).

Ezekiel 18:4 says, *"The soul who sins is the one who will die."* When sin is conceived and becomes full-grown, it produces death (see James 1:15). God is just; He must punish sin. If someone were to commit a crime, they would have to pay the penalty. Because of one man's disobedience, sin entered the world. God created the law to reveal to His people their need for a Savior. They had to sacrifice the blood of bulls and goats to be forgiven of their sins. Then Christ came onto the scene as the *Lamb of God.* He was without spot or wrinkle—He took our punishment as He hung on the cross. If we receive Him as Lord and Savior we step into the finished work of the cross. The word *redeemed* means *to be bought with a price.* We were purchased with the very blood of Jesus. Jesus gave us His Spirit and, as our Example, showed us how to live in complete obedience to God. Scripture says that Jesus was tempted with every temptation, yet never sinned (see Heb. 4:15). Through Christ, we have everything we need to live victoriously over sin.

The devil is given more credit than he deserves. We have an adversary, the devil, who is like a lion, coming to steal, kill, and destroy. We shouldn't be ignorant of his schemes, but we shouldn't fear him either. When Adam sinned, he gave the keys that God had given him over to Satan. In the desert, Satan offered to give Jesus back the keys if He would only bow down and worship him.

"The devil led him up to a high place and showed him in an instant all the kingdoms of the world. And he said to him, 'I will give you all their authority

and splendor, for it has been given to me, and I can give it to anyone I want to. So if you worship me, it will all be yours'" (Luke 4:5-7).

Satan actually had the authority at this time to give to Jesus. But luckily Jesus didn't worship him. Instead, Jesus got the keys to the kingdom back another way: He died on the cross as a Spotless Lamb, defeating the devil and his kingdom, completely overcoming sin and death. Jesus meant what He cried out on the cross, "It is finished!"

"...having canceled the written code, with its regulations, that was against us and that stood opposed to us; he took it away, nailing it to the cross. And having disarmed the powers and authorities, he made a public spectacle of them, triumphing over them by the cross" (Col. 2:14-15).

Every power and authority has been made a public spectacle by the cross. The only authority the enemy has over our lives is the authority that we give him. Sin can open the door for the enemy to wreak havoc in our lives. A good example of this in Old Testament when the Lord told the children of Israel to eat the Passover Lamb, apply the blood over the door posts, and stay in the house. But if they disobeyed God, and stepped out of the house, the death angel would kill them (see Ex. 12:22-23). We need to stay covered by the blood.

The way the enemy attacks us is primarily through our minds. The Bible is clear that when we confess our sins, Jesus is faithful and just to forgive us (see 1 John 1:9). Sometimes even after we ask forgiveness, we find ourselves stumbling back into the same sin. The enemy can try to put a snare in our souls, keeping us in habitual sin.

"I will not speak with you much longer, for the prince of this world is coming. He has no hold on me..." (John 14:29-30).

The enemy couldn't put a snare in Jesus because He had no attachment to this world. Even though the devil can put a snare in our hearts, we can't blame him for our sin. "The devil made me do it," is not a good excuse. The Bible clearly defines where our desires come from and how we are led into sin.

"...but each one is tempted when, by his own evil desire, he is dragged away and enticed. Then, after desire has conceived, it gives birth to sin; and sin, when it is full-grown, gives birth to death" (James 1:13-15).

The blood of Jesus not only has power to forgive sin, but to completely wipe it away—like it never happened—completely restoring the standard. A great example of this is after King David sinned with Bathsheba. Nathan the prophet brought David a corrective word causing him to repent.

"Then David said to Nathan, 'I have sinned against the LORD.' Nathan replied, 'The LORD has taken away your sin. You are not going to die'" (2 Sam. 12:13).

As soon as King David confessed his sin to Nathan, the Lord forgave him. But David goes on to confess his sin to the Lord—this is a great passage of Scripture:

"Have mercy on me, O God, according to your unfailing love; according to your great compassion blot out my transgressions. Wash away all my iniquity and cleanse me from my sin. For I know my transgressions, and my sin is always before me. Against you, you only, have I sinned and done what is evil in your sight, so that you are proved right when you speak and justified when you judge" (Ps. 51:1-4).

God had already forgiven King David according to II Samuel 12:13. David, however, continued to humble himself before his God and asked Him to not only forgive and blot out his transgressions, but for his heart to be made completely new:

"Create in me a pure heart, O God, and renew a steadfast spirit within me. Do not cast me from your presence or take your Holy Spirit from me. Restore to me the joy of your salvation and grant me a willing spirit, to sustain me" (Ps. 51:10-12).

The blood of Jesus has power to justify, which means to be declared righteous or acquitted. It's like we have committed a terrible crime and are standing before the judge, but because of what Jesus did on the cross the judge says, "You are forgiven!" Moreover, the blood of Jesus not only has power to forgive, but also transform—washing away any sin that tries to attach itself to our hearts—making us new. The enemy will always fight this truth. When you sin, he'll try to make you feel like God doesn't love you anymore or there is no forgiveness: "You ran out of chances!" The enemy will come with guilt, shame, and condemnation. This is a lie, and is not God. God is your Father who loves you, and wants to take you back.

> *"Then the man and his wife heard the sound of the LORD God as he was walking in the garden in the cool of the day, and they hid from the LORD God among the trees of the garden. But the LORD God called to the man, 'Where are you?' He answered, 'I heard you in the garden, and I was afraid because I was naked; so I hid'"* (Gen. 3:8-10).

After Adam and Eve are deceived by the enemy and sin, their first reaction is fear. Sin opens the door to fear. Fear is faith, but not in God. When we fear something we are saying that it has more power to affect our lives than God Himself. I heard a man once say, "If we don't overcome the fear of death, we will never live." Fear will keep us from entering into the promises of God. There are millions of scientifically proven fears: spiders, heights, the dark, etc. I've even heard of the fear of women! The enemy will always use fear as a tactic. Jesus gives us the answer, *"There is no fear in love. But perfect love drives out fear..."* (1 John 4:18). As we allow the love of God to penetrate our hearts, all of our fears will leave.

After Adam and Eve sinned they hid from God. Sin often makes us feel like we should hide from God. At the end of the story we see the first sacrifice: God clothed Adam and Eve with the skin of animals. This was prophetic of the ultimate sacrifice: Jesus on the cross. His blood covers us, giving us no reason to ever hide from God again.

> *"Let us then approach the throne of grace with confidence, so that we may receive mercy and find grace to help us in our time of need"* (Heb. 4:16).

When we stand before the Lord, He sees us through the blood of His Son, Jesus. In the Song of Solomon, it says that Solomon (who is a type and shadow of the Lord) has dove's eyes. Doves have no peripheral vision; they can only see directly ahead. The scripture goes on to say that his eyes are washed in milk; this represents purity (see Song 5:12). The wrath of God came upon Jesus so we can go on living as if we never sinned. Sin should have no dominion over us—we have been made new (see 2 Cor. 5:17). We must see ourselves that way.

Like we talked about earlier, in Paul's letter to the church in Corinth, he calls them saints. He then goes on to say the horrible things that are taking place among them. Our identity is no longer found in being sinner, but in saints who occasionally sin. There is a huge difference! I am a Son of God, washed in the blood—forgiven. This revelation will produce a desire in God's people to pursue holiness. Love is the more excellent way. I am blown away by the revelation that while we were still sinners, Christ died for us (see Rom. 5:8). When I was in my worst spiritual condition, the Lord loved me so much He died for me. God loves you just the way you are. His love will change us; He is at work in us, producing Christ-likeness. I can recall people quoting this scripture to me to put the fear of God in me. *"Therefore, my dear friends, as you have always obeyed-not only in my presence, but now much more in my absence-continue to work out your salvation with fear and trembling..."* (Phil. 2:12). If they would have only added the next verse: *"...for it is God who works in you to will and to act according to his good purpose"* (vs. 13).

Most of my Christian walk I've spent trying to crucify myself, trying to kill my flesh. Finally I had a revelation that Jesus died on the cross, not only for me, but as me. My old man died on the cross when I asked Jesus to come into my heart. That guy is dead and buried. I am a new creation, I have been set free, and I have been made new!

> *"Since, then, you have been raised with Christ, set your hearts on things above, where Christ is seated at the right hand of God. Set your minds on things above, not on earthly things. For you died, and your life is now hidden with Christ in God. When Christ, who is your life, appears, then you also will appear with him in glory. Put to death, therefore, whatever belongs to your earthly nature: sexual immorality, impurity, lust, evil desires and greed, which is idolatry. Because of these, the wrath of God is coming. You used to walk in these ways, in the life you once lived. But now you must rid yourselves of all such things as these: anger, rage, malice, slander, and filthy language from your lips. Do not lie to each other, since you have taken*

off your old self with its practices and have put on the new self, which is being renewed in knowledge in the image of its Creator" (Col. 3:1-10).

Keys to Walking in Victory over Sin

When I first was saved I had a very difficult time with the fact that Jesus laid down His entire Deity, coming to earth as a man, and was able to live His whole life without sin (see Phil. 2:5-8). I thought, "Surely that's impossible!" One day in prayer I asked the Lord to explain to me how He was able to live without sinning. I wasn't expecting a response, but immediately I heard the Lord say, "That's easy, I love My Father so much, and I would never do anything to hurt Him." Love is what keeps us from sin. When we understand the amount of suffering Christ experienced on the cross for us, and how sin hurts His heart even more, we'll sin less, not out of duty or religious obligation, but out of love. The entire law is summed up in loving God with all of our hearts and loving our neighbor as ourselves.

The second thing the Lord told me was that He knew His calling. The Bible says, *"...who for the joy set before him endured the cross"* (Heb. 12:2). Jesus had His eyes fixed on the joy set before Him. He knew that when He died on the cross and His blood was shed, those who would call upon His Name would be reconciled back to His Father. Having an understanding of the calling God has placed upon our lives is extremely important in walking victoriously over sin. Remember, without vision people perish (see Prov. 29:18). God's people are created for a purpose. If you find yourself struggling with sin, maybe you need to ask God what is it that He is calling you to do. Frequently people focus so much on their weaknesses and failures, their problems just seem to increase. In Romans 7, Paul speaks of the wrestle between the spirit and the flesh. He then asks a question in verse 24: *"Who will rescue me from this body of death?"* The next line gives the answer: *"Thanks be to God—through Jesus Christ our Lord"* (vs. 25)! Let's keep our eyes fixed on Jesus, continually coming to the throne of grace for help in time of need.

Reflection Questions

1. Explain how sin first entered the world.

_____

_____

_____

_____

_____

2. How did Jesus get back the keys to the kingdom?

_____

_____

_____

_____

_____

3. What are some things the blood of Jesus does?

_____

_____

_____

_____

_____

4. What are a few keys that help us overcome sin?

_____

_____

_____

_____

_____

- NOTES -

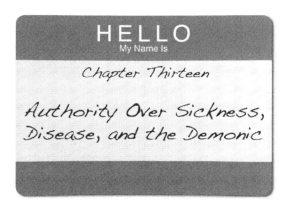

"When evening came, many who were demon-possessed were brought to him, and he drove out the spirits with a word and healed all the sick" (Matt. 8:16).

Like we discussed earlier, Jesus is our example—we are being transformed into His likeness. We are called to continue the work and ministry of Jesus on earth because we are His body—the very body of Christ. Two consistent things we find Jesus doing throughout His ministry, which will be the core subject matter of this chapter, are healing the sick and casting out demons. However, before we dive into the 'how to...' of the healing and deliverance ministry, it's necessary to understand the nature of God concerning these topics.

Many people don't have a problem with believing that it's Jesus' desire to heal people—we witness numerous accounts of this throughout Jesus' entire earthly ministry. Much of the church, however, views God the Father as Someone who would, for the sake of discipline, give His children some type of sickness or disease. This incorrect view of the nature of God can actually hinder us from being healed and delivered by a God who loves us and wants to touch us with His healing power. I've heard many physically sick Christians say concerning their illness, "This is my cross in life... this is something God wants me to bear." Sorry guys, it's not *your cross*; Jesus took our sicknesses and infirmities upon Himself, on *His cross*, so we don't have to (see Isa. 53:4-5). God the Father is our Healer. In the very heart of God, in His very nature, exists His desire to heal. Even way back in the Old Testament, God reveals to Moses and the children of Israel that He is their Healer: *"...for I am the LORD, who heals you"* (Ex. 15:26).

People tend to perceive the nature of God the Father and nature of Jesus Christ differently in many ways. But in reality, Jesus is the nature of God. If you want to see the nature of God, look at Jesus—Jesus is God the Father revealed to humanity. Jesus said it wonderfully in John 14:9—*"Anyone who has seen me has seen the Father."* We find the healing nature of God revealed in the Person of Jesus Christ. *"This Son perfectly mirrors God, and is stamped with God's nature"* (Heb. 1:3 The Message). It's essential that we catch this: *"Christ is the visible image of the invisible God... For God in all his fullness was pleased to live in Christ..."* (Col. 1:15, 19 NLT).

> *"If you, then, though you are evil, know how to give good gifts to your children, how much more will your Father in heaven give good gifts to those who ask him"* (Matt. 7:11).

God is the perfect Father. I have two sons and it's my heart's desire to see them blessed and walk in wholeness. The above verse expresses a comparison between earthly fathers and our heavenly Father—our heavenly Father is perfect. God not only loves us, but He is Love (see 1 John 4:16). Look how Paul describes love to the church in Corinth:

> *"Love is patient, love is kind. It does not envy, it does not boast, it is not proud. It is not rude, it is not self-seeking, it is not easily angered, it keeps no record of wrongs. Love does not delight in evil but rejoices with the truth. It always protects, always trusts, always hopes, always perseveres"* (1 Cor. 13:4-7).

It is the Father's desire that His children have a revelation of how much He loves us and wants us whole. A reformation is beginning in the church concerning the nature of God and how much He loves us. This reformation will produce on-fire, radical harvesters for God's kingdom. God wants to reveal Himself to us as our Savior, Provider, Healer, Deliver, Friend, Father, and much more—He is our everything.

The Greek word *Sozo* can be translated into many different English words: *save, heal, deliver, prosper, life,* and *wholeness.* The word *Sozo* is where we get the word salvation. Many people believe salvation is being saved from hell and being able to get into heaven when we die—this is true, but incomplete. When it talks about salvation in the Bible, it refers to us not only being saved from hell, but being made whole here on earth. True salvation is being filled with life, being set free, being healed, being prospered—being made whole.

The greatest miracle is salvation of our spirits, but if Jesus wants to give us the total package, I'm not going to turn it down. For me and my family, I want *everything* that Jesus paid for on the cross. There have been many times while praying for the sick that I've felt as though I had no faith and anointing. But according to God's Word I would lay hands on the sick and they would recover—many of those times they did. Our responsibility is to pray for the sick; the Lord's responsibility is to heal them.

So if God doesn't cause sickness, who does? God's original intension was to have a people set apart for Himself—a people who walked with Him, co-laboring with Him, to take dominion over the earth and establish His kingdom. When He first created mankind, there was no sickness, disease, illness, demonic oppression, or sin on the earth. But after the fall of man, after disobedience, sin entered the world—causing sickness and death to permeate all of creation. Sickness happens because we live in a fallen world—however, through Christ we are able to restore creation to wholeness.

There is another factor we need to consider as part of the equation: Satan and the realm of the demonic. Jesus said in John 10:10—*"The thief comes only to steal and kill and destroy; I have come that they may have life, and have it to the full."* In this verse we are made aware of both Jesus' résumé and Satan's. Satan's job is the killing, stealing, and destroying—we see him during the fall deceiving Eve in the garden. Jesus, on the other hand, is the one who gives abundant life. Satan and demons are closely linked with sickness, disease, sin, etc. Sickness comes from the kingdom of darkness, not from the kingdom of light. Those afflicted with sickness are under oppression of the demonic realm—not because God wants them sick.

> *"...how God anointed Jesus of Nazareth with the Holy Spirit and power, and how he went around doing good and healing all who were under the power of the devil, because God was with him"* (Acts 10:38).

It's clear that the Lord wants to heal us, delivers us, prosper us, and make us whole.

"Beloved, I pray that you may prosper in all things and be in health, just as your soul prospers" (3 John 1:2 NKJV).

The Lord teaches us to pray *"...your kingdom come, your will be done on earth as it is in heaven"* (Matt. 6:10). There is no sickness in God's kingdom. By faith and prayer, we are called to demonstrate heaven on earth. Healing is the children's bread; it's the inheritance of the saints. We must be convinced that God is, and always will be, Jehovah Rapha, the Lord who heals (see Ex. 15:26). Hebrews 13:8 says, *"Jesus Christ is the same yesterday and today and forever."* If Jesus healed people while He walked the earth, He is still healing people today! How then, do we access Christ's healing power?

"Surely he took up our infirmities and carried our sorrows, yet we considered him stricken by God, smitten by him, and afflicted. But he was pierced for our transgressions, he was crushed for our iniquities; the punishment that brought us peace was upon him, and by his wounds we are healed" (Isa. 53:4-5).

This passage is describing the crucifixion, and how on the cross the Lord took our infirmities, sorrows, transgressions, iniquities, and punishment. This verse says by His wounds we are healed. It's our responsibility as Christians to give Jesus the reward due His sufferings. For most of us, the single hope the gospel offers is being saved from hell and spending eternity with God in heaven. If that were all He did for us, that would still be enough, but our Lord decided He would do more than that. He would also heal our bodies, heal our broken hearts, set us free from bondage, and make us whole. Remember, Jesus went around doing *'good'* and healing all who were under the power of the devil. Healings and miracles flow from the goodness of God's heart toward us. Because we are children of God, His goodness freely flows upon our lives—we have access to healing through the cross. Jesus also gives us authority to heal the sick and cast out demons.

"He called his twelve disciples to him and gave them authority to drive out evil spirits and to heal every disease and sickness" (Matt. 10:1).

The Word of God is a higher truth than our present experience. *"God is not man, that he should lie..."* (Num. 23:19). If the Bible says that we have authority over sickness and disease, then why do people still get sick? This is a great question that I don't have an answer for. I can only look to Scripture and realize that my faith isn't perfect yet. Instead of forming a theology that says God doesn't heal anymore, based entirely on personal experience, we need to stand on the Word of God and keep pressing in for greater breakthrough. We have an adversary called the devil; he is fighting to keep us from walking in the fullness of what Christ paid for on the cross.

We shouldn't get discouraged if people aren't healed when we pray for them. We must continue contending for breakthrough. The Bible speaks of the *gifts* of healing and miracles. Miracles happen instantaneously: "I was blind but now I see!" I love it when God releases miracles, but there are times when He chooses to heal people. The definition of *healing* is *gradual cure or therapy*. I have seen people start to feel the pain go away, but because it isn't instant they lose faith and the enemy steals the seed. I have found that in the healing ministry it's very important to share testimonies of what God has done.

> *"They overcame him by the blood of the Lamb and by the word of their testimony..."* (Rev. 12:11).

We overcome the enemy by the blood of Jesus and the word of our testimony. As we share what God has done for us in front of people, it creates faith to rise in people to lay hold of their healing. If the enemy tries to bring the symptoms back, people who have witnessed God's healing power can say, "I had cancer, and now I'm cancer free; we will stand with you to see you healed." That testimony of God's healing power causes faith to increase in the atmosphere.

When I was six months old in the Lord, I began traveling to several third world countries with a healing evangelist. We saw many healings and miracles. One of the manifestations of God's Spirit that we regularly witnessed in the meetings was demonic manifestations—I had never observed anything like it before.

> *"But if I drive out demons by the Spirit of God, then the kingdom of God has come upon you"* (Matt. 12:28).

I'll never forget a particular meeting in Salt Lake City, Utah, where I discovered Matthew 12:28. Somehow I misunderstood the scripture and thought it meant that if I had not cast out a devil, I wasn't really saved! I asked the Lord to allow me to cast out a devil so I could be assured that I was truly born again. That night in the meeting the first few people I prayed for manifested demons—I cast them out. I was relieved; I then knew I was truly saved!

I have found that during a meeting if someone gets healed, other people often doubt that they were even sick. However, when the power of God for deliverance manifests, it's difficult for people to hold onto their unbelief. When the kingdom of God enters a meeting, it's as if all the lights turn on and all the darkness flees.

People often ask me why we don't see more deliverance in the church today. Let's look deeply into the scripture below for an answer. Jesus and three of His disciples have an encounter called the *Mount of Transfiguration*. They come down the mountain to a large crowd around the other disciples. Let's pick the story up from there:

> *"'What are you arguing with them about?' he asked. A man in the crowd answered, 'Teacher, I brought you my son, who is possessed by a spirit that has robbed him of speech. Whenever it seizes him, it throws him to the ground. He foams at the mouth, gnashes his teeth and becomes rigid. I asked your disciples to drive out the spirit, but they could not.' 'O unbelieving generation,' Jesus replied, 'how long shall I stay with you? How long shall I put up with you? Bring the boy to me.' So they brought him. When the spirit saw Jesus, it immediately threw the boy into a convulsion. He fell to the ground and rolled around, foaming at the mouth. Jesus asked the boy's father, 'How long has he been like this?' 'From childhood,' he answered. 'It has often thrown him into fire or water to kill him. But if you can do anything, take pity on us and help us.' "'If you can'?' said Jesus. 'Everything is possible for him who believes.' Immediately the boy's father exclaimed, 'I do believe; help me overcome my unbelief"* (Mark 9:16-24).

When the father tells Jesus that the disciples couldn't cast the devil out, Jesus responds by saying, "O unbelieving generation...." The context of this story is that the disciples couldn't cast the devil out because of unbelief. Let's look at the same account in Matthew 17 to see if we can get a clearer understanding from a different perspective.

"When they came to the crowd, a man approached Jesus and knelt before him. 'Lord, have mercy on my son,' he said. 'He has seizures and is suffering greatly. He often falls into the fire or into the water. I brought him to your disciples, but they could not heal him.' 'O unbelieving and perverse generation,' Jesus replied, 'how long shall I stay with you? How long shall I put up with you? Bring the boy here to me.' Jesus rebuked the demon, and it came out of the boy, and he was healed from that moment. Then the disciples came to Jesus in private and asked, 'Why couldn't we drive it out?' He replied, 'Because you have so little faith. I tell you the truth, if you have faith as small as a mustard seed, you can say to this mountain, "Move from here to there" and it will move. Nothing will be impossible for you'" (Matt. 17:14-20).

When the disciples ask Jesus why they weren't able to cast out the demon, it's very clear by Jesus' response that one of the reasons was their unbelief. In the verse below, Jesus clarifies a way that they would have been able to cast it out.

"And when He had come into the house, His disciples asked Him privately, 'Why could we not cast it out?' So He said to them, 'This kind can come out by nothing but prayer and fasting'" (Mark 9:28-29 NKJV).

Prayer and fasting increases both authority and faith for healing the sick and casting out demons. By spending time in the Lord's presence and feasting upon His Word, faith begins to increase. In the box on the following page you'll find some scriptures to meditate on that will help increase your faith and authority over the demonic.

Authority over the Demonic

"When Jesus had called the Twelve together, he gave them power and authority to drive out ALL demons and to cure diseases..." (Luke 9:1, emphasis mine).

"Jesus went up on a mountainside and called to him those he wanted, and they came to him. He appointed twelve-designating them apostles-that they might be with him and that he might send them out to preach and to have authority to drive out demons" (Mark 3:13-15).

"And these signs will accompany those who believe: In my name they will drive out demons... they will place their hands on sick people, and they will get well" (Mark 16:17-18).

"The seventy-two returned with joy and said, 'Lord, even the demons submit to us in your name.' He replied, 'I saw Satan fall like lightning from heaven. I have given you authority to trample on snakes and scorpions and to overcome all the power of the enemy; nothing will harm you. However, do not rejoice that the spirits submit to you, but rejoice that your names are written in heaven'" (Luke 10:17-20).

"He called his twelve disciples to him and gave them authority to drive out evil spirits and to heal every disease and sickness" (Matt. 10:1).

Jesus said that He only did what He saw the Father doing in heaven (see John 5:19). Our authority in Christ is not to be used presumptuously. In the healing and deliverance ministry, it's very important that we be sensitive to the leading of the Holy Spirit.

For us to understand our function as believers, it's important to be in relationship with the body of Christ. The centurion servant understood the way authority functioned because he also was one under authority. The enemy would love to get us alone and pick us off. *"...But in a multitude of counselors there is safety"* (Prov. 11:14 NKJV). In the following section, *A Call to War,* we will learn about the Lord's end-time army and how to walk together in unity and love. When we come together as the body of Christ and walk in unity, we will better understand our own personal calling and function in God's army.

Reflection Questions

1. List five Scripture references below that reveal God's nature to heal.

_____

_____

_____

_____

_____

2. What does the Greek word *Sozo* mean?

_____

_____

_____

_____

_____

3. Explain why we have authority over sickness and the demonic.

_____

_____

_____

_____

_____

4. What are some ways we overcome the enemy?

_____

_____

_____

_____

_____

- NOTES -

Part 4
A Call to War

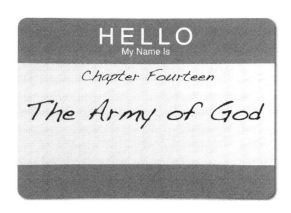

HELLO
My Name Is

Chapter Fourteen

The Army of God

The designation given to Jesus, more than any other in Scripture, is the *Lord of Hosts*. The hosts are the armies of Israel, but also the angelic forces. *Lord of Hosts* can accurately be translated as *Lord of angel armies*—our God is a warrior.

> *"Now when Joshua was near Jericho, he looked up and saw a man standing in front of him with a drawn sword in his hand. Joshua went up to him and asked, 'Are you for us or for our enemies?' 'Neither,' he replied, 'but as commander of the army of the LORD I have now come.' Then Joshua fell facedown to the ground in reverence, and asked him, 'What message does my Lord have for his servant?' The commander of the LORD'S army replied, 'Take off your sandals, for the place where you are standing is holy.' And Joshua did so. Now Jericho was tightly shut up because of the Israelites. No one went out and no one came in"* (Josh. 5:13-6:1).

We know by looking at this scripture that this was none other than the Lord Himself. Throughout Scripture, when people would bow to worship angels, the angels would tell them to stand. The only one to receive our worship is Jesus. The revelation of the church being the army of God is very important. An army goes into battle, fighting the enemy and taking ground. We have an adversary, the devil, who is trying to keep us from taking ground for the kingdom of heaven. There are some controversies around the topic of *God's army* because the gospel is about love. However, the Bible is clear that we don't fight against flesh and blood. Our war is not with one another, but with the demonic spirits in the heavens. There have been many prophetic words regarding the emerging of the army of God.

Prophecies about the Army of God

"God has given us a vision to see the body of Christ move from being an inactive audience to a Spirit-filled army . . . God is about to unloose a powerful outpouring of the Holy Spirit of an unprecedented magnitude . . . He is looking for individuals who will be 'dread champions' for his cause."

-John Wimber

"No prophet or apostle, who ever lived, equaled the power of these individuals in this great army of the Lord in these last days, No one ever had it, not even Elijah or Peter or Paul. No-one else enjoyed the power that is going to rest on this great army."

-Bob Jones

"The Lord said this, '...My people will rise up as an army and bring billions into the kingdom of God.'"

-Benny Hinn

"This army is unique. When this army comes, it's large and mighty. It's so mighty that there has never been anything like it before. What's going to happen now will transcend what Paul did, what David did and what Moses did..."

-Jack Deere

"There will be not only individuals, but an entire generation that will step into that anointing. Into that realm of authority on planet earth in the preaching and demonstration of power."

-Bill Johnson

"These will not be so called big shots; these will be ordinary everyday men and women boys and girls with an awesome anointing of God's presence and power upon their life. Expect to see great and mighty displays and demonstration of God's power."

-Bobby Conner

"At Christ's second coming the church will be found with the same power that the apostles and the early church possessed. The power of Pentecost is manifest in us. The Christian religion must be demonstrated the world wants to be shown. Then let God's power be manifest through us."

-Charles Parham

The Lord is assembling a mighty army in these last days—with Himself being the Chief Commander. This army is a militant force that will fight with prayer and passion. These knights will be completely sold out and set apart for the King and His kingdom—each individual knowing his place and function, walking in unity, for a purpose greater than themselves.

"The LORD will go forth like a warrior, He will arouse His zeal like a man of war. He will utter a shout, yes, He will raise a war cry" (Isa. 42:13 NASB).

Reflection Questions

1. What name is designated to the Lord more than any other in Scripture?

_____

_____

_____

_____

_____

2. Describe some characteristics of this end-time army.

_____

_____

_____

_____

_____

3. Who all is part of this army?

_____

_____

_____

_____

_____

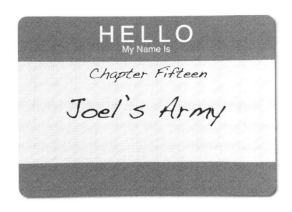

HELLO
My Name Is

Chapter Fifteen

Joel's Army

The Lord is calling together an end-time army. This army is not called to fight by way of natural means: *"For though we live in the world, we do not wage war as the world does. The weapons we fight with are not the weapons of the world"* (2 Cor. 10:3-4). Our battle is not against people, but spiritual forces in heavenly places and false views and thinking patterns (see Eph. 6:12; 2 Cor. 10:5). This army is the body of Christ—the church. There are many significant passages in Scripture that we can derive prophetic meanings concerning the army of God and apply them to our lives; such as passages found in the book of Joel. We can only understand our personal callings in relationship to others in the body of Christ.

An Increase of the Anointing

> *"...a day of darkness and gloom, a day of clouds and blackness. Like dawn spreading across the mountains a large and mighty army comes, such as never was of old nor ever will be in ages to come"* (Joel 2:2).

> *"I sent you to reap what you have not worked for. Others have done the hard work, and you have reaped the benefits of their labor"* (John 4:37-38).

We are living in the prophecy of Amos 9:13—*"'The days are coming,' declares the LORD, 'when the reaper will be overtaken by the plowman and the planter by the one treading grapes.'"* This scripture is speaking of a time of acceleration. This generation will operate on higher levels of anointing than anyone we have ever read about in history. This has nothing to do with how great the people are, but simply an increase of God's glory upon them. The Bible is very clear about this point: *""The glory of this latter temple shall be greater than the former...""* (Hag. 2:9 NKJV). This scripture doesn't say the men and women are greater—the glory is greater. Men and women have been laboring in prayer for many years, and God is answering their prayers. Years and years of laboring and persecution—this generation is walking in the breakthrough of those saints that have gone before us. The church in the book of Acts is supposed to be the floor that we step on, not the roof in that we try to attain to. According to Jesus we are going to do even greater works than Him (see John 14:12). The army God is raising up is an army of harvesters sold out for the harvest.

Unity in the Army

"They charge like warriors; they scale walls like soldiers. They all march in line, not swerving from their course. They do not jostle each other; each marches straight ahead" (Joel 2:7-8).

In a normal army there are different ranks and soldiers that line up accordingly. A private would never stand where a superior officer is supposed to be. Each person's position is very clear. Likewise, this is the way it's supposed to be in the church. We are to know our calling and not jostle with others for position. If only 20% of a human body were to function properly, it wouldn't be good for much of anything. It's important for each individual in the body of Christ to begin to understand his own personal call. As a result, the body will become more capable to function as a whole.

"I keep asking that the God of our Lord Jesus Christ, the glorious Father, may give you the Spirit of wisdom and revelation, so that you may know him better. I pray also that the eyes of your heart may be enlightened in order that you may know the hope to which he has called you, the riches of his glorious inheritance in the saints" (Eph. 1:17-18).

Paul prayed that the church would have the Spirit of wisdom and revelation for the purpose of knowing the Lord better. Remember, having a revelation of who He is, releases a revelation of who we are in Him. Paul goes on and prays that the eyes of our hearts would be opened so that we would know the hope to which He has called us. The NKJV of the Bible says, *"Where there is no vision people perish"* (Prov. 29:18). The NIV describes it this way: *"Where there is no revelation, the people cast off restraint...."* The mental image is people wandering aimlessly without vision. I have heard from horse owners that if horses are corralled together for long periods of time, they'll begin to fight with each other. I think this is true for people as well. We were not created to be corralled and wander aimlessly. We needed to be girded up for war.

I've found that people who are busy doing the work of the kingdom have less time to complain about foolish things. In the spirit I've witnessed a demonic assignment against God's people. I was in prayer when I saw what appeared to be some strange looking bird perched in the heavens. The creature would spit darts from its mouth aiming for the backs of God's people. When the darts hit the people they would, in return, spit darts out of their own mouths. The Lord showed me the darts were gossip, slander, and backbiting. The effect of the poisonous darts caused the hearts of these people to grow cold and bitter. It's interesting that in Ephesians 6:11-17 there is no armor for our backs. It's likely there's more than a single reason for this, but I believe one possibility is our brothers and sisters should be protecting our backs. The Lord longs for the body of Christ to function as one man in unity.

"The hand of the LORD was upon me, and he brought me out by the Spirit of the LORD and set me in the middle of a valley; it was full of bones. He led me back and forth among them, and I saw a great many bones on the floor of the valley, bones that were very dry. He asked me, 'Son of man, can these bones live?' I said, 'O Sovereign LORD, you alone know.' Then he said to me, 'Prophesy to these bones and say to them, "Dry bones, hear the word of the LORD! This is what the Sovereign LORD says to these bones: I will make breath enter you, and you will come to life. I will attach tendons to you and make flesh come upon you and cover you with skin; I will put breath in you, and you will come to life. Then you will know that I am the LORD."' So I prophesied as I was commanded. And as I was prophesying, there was a noise, a rattling sound, and the bones came together, bone to bone. I looked, and tendons and flesh appeared on them and skin covered them, but there was no breath in them. Then he said to me, 'Prophesy to the breath; prophesy, son of man, and say to it, "This is what the Sovereign LORD says: Come from the four winds, O breath, and breathe into these slain, that they

may live."' So I prophesied as he commanded me, and breath entered them; they came to life and stood up on their feet-a vast army" (Ez. 37:1-10).

Contextually this passage of scripture is speaking of the house of Israel although I believe it still has significance to us today. The Bible says we are one body in Christ—many members, but one body (see Rom. 12:4-5). Like in the vision, Ezekiel saw that if we are scattered, we are without life. The eye can't function without the brain, etc. We need to join together, the result being life. Unity seems impossible, but we don't have to worry. It will happen because Jesus prayed it.

"...that all of them may be one, Father, just as you are in me and I am in you" (John 17:21).

Unity is not conformity. I've been in several *unity meetings* where Christians are not allowed to pray in tongues and worship to hymns only. That's conformity, not unity. Of course I love seeing the body of Christ come together, so I will continue to attend those gatherings when invited. But true unity is *unity in diversity*. In the Old Testament we see that there were 12 tribes in the house of Israel. Each tribe had its own unique calling. This is applicable for the church today. In the New Testament, God calls us living stones (1 Peter 2:5). It's interesting that God doesn't call us bricks. Bricks all look the same; symbolically speaking of conformity. But we are living stones, having different shapes and sizes—this is what makes the body of Christ so beautiful. I believe one of the keys to unity is found in communion.

"Is not the cup of thanksgiving for which we give thanks a participation in the blood of Christ? And is not the bread that we break a participation in the body of Christ? Because there is one loaf, we, who are many, are one body, for we all partake of the one loaf" (1 Cor. 10:15-17).

"In the following directives I have no praise for you, for your meetings do more harm than good. In the first place, I hear that when you come together as a church, there are divisions among you, and to some extent I believe it. No doubt there have to be differences among you to show which of you have God's approval. When you come together, it is not the Lord's Supper you eat,

for as you eat, each of you goes ahead without waiting for anybody else. One remains hungry, another gets drunk. Don't you have homes to eat and drink in? Or do you despise the church of God and humiliate those who have nothing? What shall I say to you? Shall I praise you for this? Certainly not! For I received from the Lord what I also passed on to you: The Lord Jesus, on the night he was betrayed, took bread, and when he had given thanks, he broke it and said, 'This is my body, which is for you; do this in remembrance of me.' In the same way, after supper he took the cup, saying, 'This cup is the new covenant in my blood; do this, whenever you drink it, in remembrance of me.' For whenever you eat this bread and drink this cup, you proclaim the Lord's death until he comes. Therefore, whoever eats the bread or drinks the cup of the Lord in an unworthy manner will be guilty of sinning against the body and blood of the Lord. A man ought to examine himself before he eats of the bread and drinks of the cup. For anyone who eats and drinks without recognizing the body of the Lord eats and drinks judgment on himself. That is why many among you are weak and sick, and a number of you have fallen asleep. But if we judged ourselves, we would not come under judgment." (1 Cor. 11:17:31).

Communion is a time for God's people to come together in remembrance of the Lord and His death until He returns. In this verse it's interesting to see that people became sick for not properly examining the Lord's body while taking communion. This is not speaking of improperly examining the loaf of bread, or even the physical body of Jesus. This scripture is speaking of properly examining the body of Christ and your relationship to the body of Christ.

What is going to bring arguing denominations into unity? The answer is the broken body and shed blood of Jesus Christ. All denominations that believe that Jesus Christ died on the cross, rose from the dead, was born of a virgin, was the only begotten Son of God, and is the only way to salvation all agree on the most important things. We have, as Christians, the one thing that will bring us together—the broken body and shed blood of Jesus Christ. I don't need to try to get Baptists to speak in tongues, or tell the Charismatics to stop lifting their hands in worship. The common union (communion) that we all possess as children of God is what Jesus did on the cross for us.

Reflection Questions

1. If we don't wrestle against flesh and blood, who then is our battle against?

_____

_____

_____

_____

_____

2. Why is unity in the body of Christ so important?

_____

_____

_____

_____

_____

3. Explain why we are called *living stones* and not *bricks*.

_____

_____

_____

_____

_____

4. What is our *common union* as believers?

_____

_____

_____

_____

_____

Part 5
Living in the Supernatural

Once you were alienated from God and were enemies in your minds because of your evil behavior (Col. 1:21).

According to Scripture, our minds are what alienate us from God. Jesus was crucified on Mt. Golgotha, otherwise known as the *place of skulls* (see Mark 15:22). The mountain itself looks like a huge skull. The cross pierced the skull. This is a type and shadow of the cross having the power to renew our minds.

"The weapons we fight with are not the weapons of the world. On the contrary, they have divine power to demolish strongholds. We demolish arguments and every pretension that sets itself up against the knowledge of God, and we take captive every thought to make it obedient to Christ" (2 Cor. 10:3-6).

The battle is in our minds. Our minds are like computers; although our spirits have been born again, our minds remember the sins we have committed in the past and still retain old ways of thinking. Our computers need to be reprogrammed. Strongholds in our minds hinder us from stepping into the destiny God has called us into; arguments are the defense mechanisms that keep them there.

Strongholds are formed as early as childhood. A little child's mind is like fertile soil—whatever seeds are planted will grow if watered—both good and bad seeds. The bad seeds (negative words) grow into large trees if they're not dealt with. The only way to remove a stronghold is by the root. The Bible says, *"You shall know the truth and the truth shall make you free"* (John 8:32). The key to destroying strongholds in our lives is to replace them with truth. Arguments and excuses against the truth are the defense mechanisms that keep the stronghold in place.

For example, I once heard a story of two little girls walking to school one morning. One little girl said to the other, "If I can't put my fingers around your wrist, and make a bracelet, you are fat." The little girl was smaller than the other and couldn't make a bracelet around her wrist and called her fat. Although the other girl wasn't fat, she grew up and struggled with eating disorders, always feeling like she was too fat. The smaller girl sowed a seed, and the enemy made sure it was watered. There are many things that take place like this in life. We need the light of Christ to shine in our hearts exposing the lies of the enemy.

The word *repent* means *to change the way we think*. Repentance is not a one time event, but something that we will do until the day we go to be with the Lord. Instead of defending and agreeing with the lies of the enemy, we need to *repent* and *change the way we think*— allowing our minds to come into alignment with the truth of God. Most people think repentance simply means contrition—feeling sorry for our sin. Others think it means making an about face—turning 180 degrees. The problem is turning away from something is not enough—we need to turn towards the person of Jesus Christ and allow our minds to be renewed. If we don't change the way we think, we will keep turning back to our old ways. The best definition of repentance I have heard is by breaking down the word into two parts: "re" and "pentence." *Re-* means "to go back," and *–pentence* is like "penthouse": going back to the highest place. The Bible says we are seated in heavenly places with Christ and in Christ (Eph. 2:6). When we repent we are not only forgiven, but brought into the heavenlies, the highest place with God receiving His perspective—His way of thinking!

We are triune beings: spirit, soul, and body. We are suppose to live our lives spirit first, then soul. The mind is to be the servant to the spirit-man. When the Lord speaks truth to us, our spirits receive it, but it still has to be processed by our minds. We can receive true revelation from God, but if our minds aren't renewed they will discard what the Lord speaks to us. Our minds need to be renewed and reprogrammed to believe in the eternal realm where God dwells.

You know your mind is being renewed when the impossible seems possible. Like when in the past, not having money to pay the bills brought stress—but now it brings a strange sense of excitement and expectation for God to make a miracle happen. I know people who get excited when they see someone with a cane or crutch. They believe God loves them so much, that He would put someone who needs healing right in front of them. That's not the normal way to think. Jesus said, *"What is impossible with men is possible with God"* (Luke 18:27). The Lord wants His people to believe that arms can grow back, tumors can fall off, blind eyes can be opened—to God, this is no problem.

> *"'The eye is the lamp of the body. If your eyes are good, your whole body will be full of light. But if your eyes are bad, your whole body will be full of darkness. If then the light within you is darkness, how great is that darkness'"* (Matt. 6:22-23)!

This scripture in the King James Version says if the eye be single, then the whole body is filled with light. As our eyes are single focused on the Lord, we are filled with His light. As we focus our eyes on darkness, our entire body will be filled with darkness. What we focus on is what we become like. We see this example with Jacob. He receives a revelation from the Lord to have the flocks of sheep conceive in front of the watering trough. What they looked at they became like.

> *"Jacob, however, took fresh-cut branches from poplar, almond and plane trees and made white stripes on them by peeling the bark and exposing the white inner wood of the branches. Then he placed the peeled branches in all the watering troughs, so that they would be directly in front of the flocks when they came to drink. When the flocks were in heat and came to drink, they mated in front of the branches. And they bore young that were streaked or speckled or spotted. Jacob set apart the young of the flock by themselves, but made the rest face the streaked and dark-colored animals that belonged to Laban. Thus he made separate flocks for himself and did not put them with Laban's animals. Whenever the stronger females were in heat, Jacob would place the branches in the troughs in front of the animals so they would mate near the branches, but if the animals were weak, he would not place them there. So the weak animals went to Laban and the strong ones to Jacob. In this way the man grew exceedingly prosperous and came to own*

large flocks, and maidservants and menservants, and camels and donkeys" (Gen. 30:37-43).

If we were to stand at the foot of the tallest mountain it would appear massive. However, if we looked at it from heaven's perspective, it would seem very small. As we fix our eyes upon Jesus, all of our worries don't seem to so big anymore. His glory begins to transform us—God can do the impossible.

"Let us fix our eyes on Jesus, the author and perfecter of our faith, who for the joy set before him endured the cross, scorning its shame, and sat down at the right hand of the throne of God" (Heb. 12:2).

"You will keep him in perfect peace, Whose mind is stayed on You, Because he trusts in You" (Isa. 26:3 NKJV).

In Matthew 17, we see Jesus transfigured on the mountain; He was lit up like a light bulb. The same Greek word *metamorphoo* is translated into English as transfigured and *transformed*. The other time we see this word used in the Bible is in Romans 12:2—*"Do not conform any longer to the pattern of this world, but be transformed by the renewing of your mind. Then you will be able to test and approve what God's will is-his good, pleasing and perfect will...."*

Metamorphoo NT:3339, "to change into another form" (meta, implying change, and morphe, "form:" see FORM, No. 1), is used in the passive voice (a) of Christ's "transfiguration," Matt. 17:2; Mark 9:2; Luke (in 9:29) avoids this term, which might have suggested to gentile readers the metamorphoses of heathen gods, and uses the phrase egeneto heteron, "was altered", lit., "became (ginomai) different (heteros)"; (b) of believers, Rom. 12:2, "be ye transformed," the obligation being to undergo a complete change which, under the power of God, will find expression in character and conduct; morphe lays stress on the inward change, schema (see the preceding verb in that verse, suschematizo) lays stress on the outward (see FASHION, No. 3, FORM, No. 2); the present continuous tenses indicate a process; 2 Cor 3:18 describes believers as being "transformed (RV) into the same image" (i. e., of

Christ in all His moral excellencies), the change being effected by the Holy Spirit.

(from Vine's Expository Dictionary of Biblical Words, Copyright ©1985, Thomas Nelson Publishers)

The Lord is saying the key to transformation is the renewal of the mind. It's interesting that when Adam sinned, he saw that he was naked. I believe that before the fall, Adam was radiant like Jesus was during the Mount of Transfiguration experience. We see the same thing happening under the Old Covenant with Moses. How much more is the glory supposed to radiate from those who have the indwelling Holy Spirit?

"Now if the ministry that brought death, which was engraved in letters on stone, came with glory, so that the Israelites could not look steadily at the face of Moses because of its glory, fading though it was, will not the ministry of the Spirit be even more glorious" (2 Cor. 3:7-8).

The first key to transformation and walking in the realms of the supernatural is the renewal of the mind. The second key is beholding God's glory in His Word.

"Now the Lord is the Spirit, and where the Spirit of the Lord is, there is liberty (emancipation from bondage, freedom). And all of us, as with unveiled face, [because we] continued to behold [in the Word of God] as in a mirror the glory of the Lord, are constantly being transfigured into His very own image in ever increasing splendor and from one degree of glory to another; [for this comes] from the Lord [Who is] the Spirit" (2 Cor. 3:17-18 AMP).

According to the above scripture, as we meditate on the word of God, He transforms us from glory to glory into His very image. The Bible is alive and has power to change and challenge the way we think. The Bible can be a history book, a story book, or a living book filled with power to transform. The key is meditating upon it. Meditate on one passage of scripture until it becomes alive to you. I heard a man once say, "If the Word doesn't lead to an experience with God, it will only make us religious." The Pharisees had the entire Old Testament memorized, but when Jesus, the promised Messiah, stood before them, they couldn't recognize Him. The Word must be breathed on by the Holy Spirit. We need both the Word of God and the Spirit of God to produce transformation.

"All Scripture is God-breathed and is useful for teaching, rebuking, correcting and training in righteousness, so that the man of God may be thoroughly equipped for every good work" (2 Tim. 3:16-17).

"For the word of God is living and active. Sharper than any double-edged sword, it penetrates even to dividing soul and spirit, joints and marrow; it judges the thoughts and attitudes of the heart" (Heb. 4:12).

"...to make her holy, cleansing her by the washing with water through the word..." (Eph. 5:26).

"You are already clean because of the word I have spoken to you" (John 15:3).

Encountering God also helps renew our minds. It is impossible for someone with a broken arm to be instantly healed, but nothing is impossible with God. I once ministered at a youth camp where the Lord instantly healed a young man's broken arm. That miracle will stick with those young people forever. The next time they see someone with a broken arm, they will remember what God did for that young man. That will change the way you think.

One last key to help our minds be renewed is praying in the Spirit. The Bible says, *"...the natural man does not receive the things of the Spirit of God, for they are foolishness to him; nor can he know them, because they are spiritually discerned"* (1 Cor. 2:14). As we pray in the Spirit, the more and more we are able to understand and receive the things of the Spirit of God. To the man or woman with a renewed mind, the supernatural becomes natural.

Reflection Questions

1. If we are born again, why do we still need our minds renewed?

_____

_____

_____

_____

_____

2. What does the word *repent* mean?

_____

_____

_____

_____

_____

3. When things seem impossible and the mountains in our lives seem too big, what should we do? What happens when we do?

_____

_____

_____

_____

_____

4. What are some keys talked about in this chapter that will help our minds become renewed?

_____

_____

_____

_____

_____

- NOTES -

Chapter Seventeen

Encountering God by Faith

...He awakens Me morning by morning, He awakens My ear To hear as the learned (Isa. 50:4 NKJV).

The Lord Jesus heard the voice of God daily. As sons and daughters of God, we have the privilege of hearing God's voice. As we talked about in Chapter One, Enoch *walked* with God—literally meaning he *walked up and down.* Enoch visited heaven numerous times before the Lord allowed him to stay. God is looking for a generation, like Enoch, who will walk with Him.

Whether or not we literally visit heaven is up to God. Although I believe in heavenly visitations, that's not what I'm emphasizing. I'm speaking about a people who hunger for the presence of God and the fullness of all that belongs to us as sons and daughters. There is a hunger in the heart of every believer that can only be satisfied by experiencing God. Most Christians have been taught that *experience* is not good and it's the door to deception. We do need to be carful with experience. If an angel comes to me and preaches a message that contradicts the gospel, I'm going to rebuke it—it's not from God. This is why it's critical to read the Word and understand the nature of God. With this being said, we shouldn't cast off experience altogether. Fearing experience has kept many people from experiencing God's fullness. If we don't experience God, we aren't walking in biblical Christianity. We can't make experiences with God happen. However, we should believe and have faith for them, as well as positioning ourselves in a place to receive them. God is alive and He loves us.

"[That you may really come] to know [practically, through experience for yourselves] the love of Christ, which far surpasses mere knowledge [without

experience]; that you may be filled [through all your being] unto all the fullness of God [may have the richest measure of the divine Presence, and become a body wholly filled and flooded with God Himself]" (Eph. 3:19 AMP).

This scripture says that we should come to know God, through our own experience. Listening to messages about the love of God is not the same as experiencing the love of God. Hearing about someone else's relationship with God will not satisfy our need for relationship—it's not enough.

If believers don't encounter the presence of God, discern His peace, hear His voice, and be led by His Spirit, they will only become religious. 2 Corinthians 3:6 says, *"...for the letter kills, but the Spirit gives life."* We can't even read the Bible without the life-giving Spirit of God—He's the Person who gives us life. If we are born-again believers, we have the privilege and opportunity to experience God and the entire realm of His kingdom.

"Jesus answered him, I assure you, most solemnly I tell you, that unless a person is born again (anew, from above), he cannot ever see (know, be acquainted with, and experience) the kingdom of God" (John 3:3 AMP).

The Lord wants us to experience Him like Saul did on the road to Damascus. He wants the scales from our eyes to fall off so we can see Him for who He really is. There has been a prayer in my heart since I first met the Lord: "Lord, I want to see You face to face, to experience Your presence, and to be allowed a glimpse of heaven." I realize now that this prayer is God's will for my life.

Will you dare with me to believe that we can experience God, hear His voice, and feel His presence, while here on earth? Heaven is our home, now. When Jesus cried out, "It is finished", the veil was torn from top to bottom. We have been given a way to come boldly to the throne of grace—we have access to the very presence of God.

The definition of a kiss is *to touch or caress with the lips as an act of affection, greeting, etc.* Would you rather hear the definition of a kiss, or experience one? God wants to touch us, but we must want His touch. King David exclaimed, *"As the deer pants for streams of water, so my soul pants for you, O God"* (Psalm 42:1). We are the generation that shares the same cry as Moses: "Lord, show us Your glory!" Do you know what our ministry is as believers?

> *"And all of us, as with unveiled face, [because we] continued to behold [in the Word of God] as in a mirror the glory of the Lord, are constantly being transfigured into His very own image in ever increasing splendor and from one degree of glory to another; [for this comes] from the Lord [Who is] the Spirit. THEREFORE, SINCE we do hold and engage in this ministry..."* (2 Cor. 3:18-4:1).

Paul is continuing his message from chapter three into chapter four. Our ministry is beholding the glory of God. The ministry of every believer is ministering to the Lord and beholding Him—all other things are birthed from this.

Reflection Questions

1. Why is it so important to experience God... not just hear about Him and His works?

_____

_____

_____

2. What did Jesus say was the prerequisite for seeing and experiencing the kingdom of God?

_____

_____

_____

3. What is our ministry as believers?

_____

_____

_____

_____

- NOTES -

HELLO
My Name Is

Chapter Eighteen

Citizens of Heaven

Since, then, you have been raised with Christ, set your hearts on things above, where Christ is seated at the right hand of God. Set your minds on things above, not on earthly things (Col. 3:1-2).

King David said, *"I'm a stranger on the earth"* (Ps. 119:19). Paul said that *"...our citizenship is in heaven"* (Phil. 3:20). As children of God, our minds and hearts are in heaven and our feet are on earth walking it out. Heaven is our home, now.

> *"By faith Abraham, when called to go to a place he would later receive as his inheritance, obeyed and went, even though he did not know where he was going. By faith he made his home in the promised land like a stranger in a foreign country; he lived in tents, as did Isaac and Jacob, who were heirs with him of the same promise. For he was looking forward to the city with foundations, whose architect and builder is God. All these people were still living by faith when they died. They did not receive the things promised; they only saw them and welcomed them from a distance. And they admitted that they were aliens and strangers on earth. People who say such things show that they are looking for a country of their own. If they had been thinking of the country they had left, they would have had opportunity to return. Instead, they were longing for a better country-a heavenly one. Therefore God is not ashamed to be called their God, for he has prepared a city for them"* (Heb. 11:8-10, 13-16).

Being a pilgrim on earth doesn't mean we don't have a home, a car, or any possessions—it's more than that. Being sojourner on earth is a heart attitude that says, "Take the world and give me You!" God is our Father and He desires to bless us with natural things as well as spiritual things. It's clear that as we seek first the kingdom of God, making it our primary concern, God will provide for all of our needs.

There is a hunger in the heart of every person to experience eternity (see Eccl. 3:11). Leonard Ravenhill once said, "God has burned eternity on our eyeballs." Once eternity is our focus our desires being to change—what's important to God is important to us.

Those focused on eternity are able to overcome great challenges and difficulties this world and the enemy throws at them. I've heard people say, "You're too heavenly minded to be any earthly good." The truth is if we were really heavenly minded, we would turn the world upside down. Once again, the battle is in our minds. The first step in the right direction is setting our minds, and fixing our hearts, on things that are of God.

> *"Finally, brothers, whatever is true, whatever is noble, whatever is right, whatever is pure, whatever is lovely, whatever is admirable—if anything is excellent or praiseworthy—think about such things"* (Phil. 4:8).

There are people arising on the earth today who don't let the things of the world hold them back from God and the things He is calling them to do. When I first gave my life to the Lord, I left everything behind to follow Him and travel the world to preach the gospel. People would ask me, "Why are you doing that?" It doesn't make sense to the world.

When God opens our eyes when we catch a glimpse of Him, like Saul of Tarsus, it becomes easy for us to lay our lives down for the One who laid His life down for us. The cross I carry becomes my passion as I keep my eyes fixed on Him.

Reflection Questions

1. What does it mean to be a citizen of heaven?

_____

_____

_____

_____

_____

2. Why is it so important for us to not only glimpse eternity, but to live from the eternal realm?

_____

_____

_____

_____

_____

3. What happens when we get just a glimpse of the Lord?

_____

_____

_____

_____

_____

- NOTES -

HELLO
My Name Is

Chapter Nineteen

The Mountain of The Lord

Recently I had a prophetic experience while driving my car. In the natural I could see the road in front of me, and was very conscience of the semi-flat landscape around. In the spirit, however, I saw a large mountain. Immediately I heard the voice of God say, "If this generation doesn't come to the Mountain of the Lord, they will try to put Me back in a box and put My commandments back on stone."

Following this experience, I understand that God wants His people to come to His Mountain to hear His voice. We need to listen to what the Lord is saying; it's essential that we hear His voice. Obviously we can't literally stick God in a box—we can, however, limit Him to a box in our minds. It's not as much what *He has said*, but what *He is saying*. The sober reality is our lives and future may very well rest in our aptitude for hearing and heeding what the Spirit of God is speaking to us in this hour.

The key to hearing the *voice* of God is saturating and immersing ourselves in the *presence* of God. When we come into His presence, the rest simply happens. We will, at times, confront thoughts and mindsets contrary to the will and nature of God, which are often exposed in the light of His presence. Remember, *"...whenever anyone turns to the Lord, the veil is taken away"* (2 Cor. 3:16). Clarity comes in His presence. It's important, first, to recognize these thoughts as opposing the truth, then, take them captive to the obedience of Christ. If we choose, however, not to heed the leading of the Spirit, it's possible to limit God's power and anointing from flowing through our lives because of un-renewed thinking patterns. This is why it's so important that we have the mind of Christ. Our lives will be transformed, but primarily after our minds our renewed (see Rom. 12:2).

If we do not come to the mountain of the Lord to hear His voice, we will endeavor to put His commandments back on stone—setting up religious altars and embracing old wineskins—gripping tightly the ritualistic rules and regulations of legalism. It's not so much about the do's and don'ts of Christian living, but walking in fellowship with the life-giving Christ. *"So, as the Holy Spirit says: 'Today, if you hear his voice, do not harden your hearts...'"* (Heb. 3:7-8). God is speaking *today*; can you hear what He's saying? Our daily bread is the word of God; we can't live off of yesterday's manna.

In the vision the Lord was referring to Exodus 19:5-6—*"Now if you obey me fully and keep my covenant, then out of all nations you will be my treasured possession. Although the whole earth is mine, you will be for me a kingdom of priests and a holy nation." These are the words you are to speak to the Israelites.'"* God's original intention for His people was that they would be a kingdom of priests. A priest's first responsibility is to minister to the Lord, then second, minister to God's people. God's desire is that we, a generation of priests, would come to His Mountain to speak directly with Him and hear His voice.

After Moses led the children of Israel out of slavery they approached Mt. Sinai, where God was. When God's people heard the thunder and saw the lightning, they were overwhelmed with fear and told Moses to be the mediator. This is one of the saddest passages in Scripture: *"The people remained at a distance, while Moses approached the thick darkness where God was"* (Ex. 20:21). God has never wanted only one person to approach His presence; He wants all of His children to come near Him.

Much later in the story Moses came to the base of the mountain, after encountering the Lord. He found the children of Israel making sacrifices to false gods and worshiping a golden calf they had made. The children of Israel witnessed incredible miracles done by the hand of God; yet, they still fell away. Signs, wonders, and miracles are part of our inheritance as believers; we need to continue believing and contending for greater breakthrough in this arena. However, witnessing the miraculous doesn't necessarily mean we aren't capable of losing connection with God. It is still very possible to witness God's power, and even minister under the anointing, and still fall away to worship idols. What separated Moses from the children of Israel? Why did Moses remain faithful, while the others turned away from God? The answer is found in Psalm 103:7—*"He made known his ways to Moses...."*

Moses witnessed the *power of God*, but he also learned the *ways of God*. If we don't come to intimately know the ways of God, we will always question His motives: "Can I really trust You?" When led out of slavery, the children of Israel complained because they didn't have any meat to eat like they had in Egypt. They didn't understand the ways of God, so they thought that they were being punished. In reality God was teaching them to put their trust and faith in Him. He wanted to reveal Himself as a faithful and good God who provides.

Jesus Christ is our High Priest. His blood was sprinkled on the mercy seat so we can come boldly before the throne of grace, obtaining mercy and finding grace in our time of need (see Heb. 4:16). God has made a new covenant with us through His Son Jesus, the Mediator of this new covenant.

> *"For this reason Christ is the mediator of a new covenant, that those who are called may receive the promised eternal inheritance—now that he has died as a ransom to set them free from the sins committed under the first covenant"* (Heb. 9:15).

As Jesus hung from the cross, He cried out, "It is finished!" The veil in the temple was torn from top to bottom. We now have access to the holy of holies where the presence of God dwells. As sons and daughters of God, we are invited to come into the very real, very tangible, presence of God. I used to have a difficult time understanding and believing that God wanted me to enter into His presence. I thought to myself, "God is Holy, I am not. If I go into His presence He's going to kill me, or at least be mad at me." Thankfully the Holy Spirit began to reveal to me the love of the Father—I'm God's son and He loves me, and is pleased with me. However, I also began to learn that there is a healthy type of fear of God.

> *"When the people saw the thunder and lighting and heard the trumpet and saw the mountain in smoke, they trembled with fear. They stayed at a distance and said to Moses, 'Speak to us yourself and we will listen. But do not have God speak to us or we will die.' Moses said to the people, 'Do not be afraid. God has come to test you, so that the fear of God will be with you to keep you from sinning'"* (Ex. 20:18-20).

God is Love and He is our Father. 1 John 4:18 says, *"There is no fear in love. But perfect love drives out fear, because fear has to do with punishment."* Fearing punishment comes from the enemy, not from God. The love of God drives out fear, but it doesn't drive out the fear of the Lord. There is a healthy type of fear—the fear of the Lord—which is actually for our benefit. Jesus is our example, and the fear of the Lord rested on Him; He even delighted in it (see Isa. 11:2-3).

Moses responded to the people's fear by telling them not to fear. He then goes on to say that the fear of God that is with them will keep them from sinning. *"'To fear the LORD is to hate evil...'"* (Prov. 8:13). Fearing God produces a righteous hatred of evil and an adoration for things that are pure.

To *fear the Lord* means to *revere Him* or *show Him respect.* I've been concerned with my generation regarding this issue. I've listened to several people, deep in sin, say that God knows their hearts and will love them even if they continue walking in disobedience. This is true, God will always love us, but being truly saved means we no longer want to sin because it hurts the One who loves us. A comment like that makes me wonder if the person is even saved. Paul teaches on grace in the New Testament and tells us not to use it as a license to sin (see Rom. 6:1-2).

Many people fall away from God because their relationship with Him was never their own. It's essential that every person comes to the Mountain to experience the presence of God. The story of the children of Israel proves that we can witness God's power, but if we don't know God experientially, we can fall away. Mt. Sinai was where Moses encountered the Lord. As we read above, it was a very scary sight. Look at the mountain we're invited to:

> *"But you have come to Mount Zion, to the heavenly Jerusalem, the city of the living God. You have come to thousands upon thousands of angels in joyful assembly, to the church of the firstborn, whose names are written in heaven. You have come to God, the judge of all men, to the spirits of righteous men made perfect, to Jesus the mediator of a new covenant, and to the sprinkled blood that speaks a better word than the blood of Abel"* (Heb. 12:22-24).

The blood of Abel cried out *vengeance*—the blood of Jesus cries out *mercy* and *forgiveness*. This mountain is warm and inviting—angels welcome us! Jesus is the mediator of this new covenant and has made a way for us to come into the very heart of God. The Father is inviting an entire generation to come to the Mountain of the Lord to worship Him there and hear His voice. Will you come?

Reflection Questions

1. Why is it important to hear God's voice for ourselves and not just through others?

_____

_____

_____

_____

_____

2. What does it mean to put God in a box and put His commandments back on stone?

_____

_____

_____

_____

_____

3. Why is it important to not only witness the *power* of God, but to also know the *ways* of God?

_____

_____

_____

_____

_____

4. Explain the fear of the Lord in your own words. Why is the fear of the Lord good?

_____

_____

_____

_____

_____

5. What is God inviting us to do?

_____

_____

_____

_____

_____

Appendix A

Contrasting the Orphan Heart with the Heart of Sonship

Taken from *Spiritual Slavery to Spiritual Sonship* by Jack Frost

ORPHAN HEART		HEART OF SONSHIP
See God as Master	IMAGE OF GOD	See God as a Loving Father
Independent/Self-reliant	DEPENDENCY	Interdependent/ Acknowledges Need
Live by the Love of Law	THEOLOGY	Live by the Law of Love
Insecure/Lack Peace	SECURITY	Rest and Peace
Strive for the praise, approval, and acceptance of people.	NEED FOR APPROVAL	Totally accepted in God's love and justified by grace.
A need for personal achievement as you seek to impress God and others, or no motivation to serve at all.	MOTIVE FOR SERVICE	Service that is motivated by a deep gratitude for being unconditionally loved and accepted by God.
Duty and earning God's favor or no motivation at all.	MOTIVE BEHIND CHRISTIAN DISCIPLINES	Pleasure and Delight
"Must" be holy to have God's favor, thus increasing a sense of shame and guilt	MOTIVATION FOR PURITY	"Want to" be holy; do not want anything to hinder intimate relationship with God.
Self-rejection from comparing yourself to others.	SELF-IMAGE	Positive and affirmed because you know you have such value to God.
Seek comfort in counterfeit affections: addictions, compulsions, escapism, busyness, hyper-religious activity.	SOURCE OF COMFORT	Seek times of quietness and solitude to rest in the Father's presence and love.
Competition, rivalry, and jealousy toward others' success and position.	PEER RELATIONSHIPS	Humility and unity as you value others and are able to rejoice in their blessings and success.
Accusation and exposure in order to make yourself look good by making others look bad.	HANDLING OTHERS' FAULTS	Love covers as you seek to restore others in a spirit of love and gentleness.
See authority as a source of pain; distrustful toward them and lack a heart attitude of submission.	VIEW OF AUTHORITY	Respectful, honoring: you see them as ministers of God for good in your life.

Difficulty receiving admonition; you must be right so you easily get your feelings hurt and close your spirit to discipline.	VIEW OF ADMONITION	See the receiving of admonition as a blessing and need in your life so that your faults and weaknesses are exposed and put to death
Guarded and conditional; based upon others' performance as you seek to get your own needs met.	EXPRESSION OF LOVE	Open, patient, and affectionate as you lay your life and agendas down in order to meet the needs of others.
Conditional and Distant	SENSE OF GOD'S PRESENCE	Close and Intimate
Bondage	CONDITION	Liberty
Feel like a Servant/Slave	POSITION	Feel like a Son/Daughter
Spiritual ambition; the earnest desire for some spiritual achievement and distinction and the willingness to strive for it; a desire to be seen and counted among the mature.	VISION	To daily experience the Father's unconditional love and acceptance and then be sent as a representative of His love to family and others.
Fight for what you can get!	FUTURE	Sonship releases your inheritance!

Appendix A taken from *Spiritual Slavery to Spiritual Sonship* by Jack Frost.

Frost, Jack. Spiritual Slavery to Spiritual Sonship. Shippensburg, PA: Destiny Image Publishers, Inc., 2006.

Appendix B
I am because I AM

1. I am Redeemed (Rev. 5:9)

2. I am bought with a price (1 Cor. 6:20)

3. I am Blood bought (1 Peter 1:19; Rev. 5:9)

4. I am valuable to God (Matt. 10:31)

5. I am one in which God has an inheritance (Eph. 1:18)

6. I am reconciled to God (2 Cor. 5:18)

7. I am made clean (John 13:10)

8. I am saved by the Gospel (1 Cor. 15:2)

9. I am born again of incorruptible seed (1 Peter 1:23)

10. I am a new creation (2 Cor. 5:17)

11. I am in Christ Jesus (1 Cor. 1:30)

12. I am complete in Him (Col. 2:10)

13. I am free from the control of man (1 Cor. 9:19)

14. I am free from sin (Rom. 6:18,22)

15. I am free from the law of sin and death (Rom. 8:2)

16. I am free from the curse of the law (Gal. 3:13)

17. I am free indeed (John 8:32-36)

18. I am called according to His purpose (Rom. 8:30)

19. I am called into the fellowship of His Son (1 Cor. 1:9)

20. I am called to peace (1 Cor. 7:15)

21. I am called to liberty (Gal. 5:13)

22. I am called to His eternal glory (1 Peter 5:10)

23. I am God's field (1 Cor. 3:9)

24. I am God's building (1 Cor. 3:9)

25. I am a branch connected into the Vine Jesus Christ and His life flows through me (John 15:5)

26. I am healed from every infirmity (1 Peter 2:24; Isa. 53:5)

27. I am immune from every sickness and disease (Ex. 23:25; Deut. 7:15)

28. I am an epistle of Christ, written not with ink but by the Spirit of the living God (2 Cor. 3:3)

29. I am Christ's (1 Cor. 3:23)

30. I am the Friend of God (John 15:15)

31. I am a servant of God (1 Cor. 9:19)

32. I am a part of the Body of Christ (1 Cor. 12:27)

33. I am one of the saints in Christ Jesus (Rom. 1:6; Gal. 3:28)

34. I am a fellow citizen with all the saints in the Kingdom of God (Eph. 2:19)

35. I am the temple of the Lord and the Holy Spirit dwells within me (1 Cor. 3:16, 6:19; 2 Cor. 6:16; John 14:7)

36. I am Abraham's seed (Gal. 3:29)

37. I am an heir according to the promises made to Abraham (Gal. 3:29)

38. I am part of a chosen generation (1 Peter 2:9)

39. I am a member of a royal priesthood (1 Peter 2:9)

40. I am a citizen of a holy nation (1 Peter 2:9)

41. I am one of His own special people (1 Peter 2:9)

42. I am an heir of God a joint heir with Jesus Christ (Gal. 4:7)

43. I am member of the household of God (Eph. 2:19)

44. I am a child of the most high God (Rom. 8:16; Gal. 3:26; Gal. 4:7)

45. I am a child of light (Eph. 5:8; 1 Thess. 5:8)

46. I am a child of the day (1 Thess. 5:8)

47. I am a proclaimer of the praises of Him who called me out of darkness into His marvelous light (1 Peter 2:9)

48. I am light in the Lord (Eph. 5:8)

49. I am the light of the world (Matt. 5:14)

50. I am the salt of the earth (Matt. 5:13)

51. I am blessed in the city and in the country (Deut. 28:3)

52. I am the Father/Mother of blessed children (Deut. 28:4)

53. I am blessed in all I lay my hands to (Deut. 28:4-5, 8)

54. I am blessed when I come in and when I go out (Deut. 28:6)

55. I am invincible before my enemies (Deut. 28:7)

56. I am the head and not the tail (Deut. 28:13)

57. I am above and not beneath (Deut. 28:13)

58. I am a lender not a borrower (Deut. 15:6; 28:12)

59. I am strong in the Lord (1 John 2:14)

60. I am one in whom the word of God abides (1 John 2:14)

61. I am one who has overcome the wicked one (1 John 2:14)

62. I am rich in Him (Rom. 8:32; Rev. 2:9)

63. I am gifted with powerful gifts from the Holy Ghost (1 Cor. 12:4-11)

64. I am a believer in Jesus Christ therefore I am one who casts out demons in His Name (Mark 16:17)

65. I am one who speaks with new tongues (Mark 16:17)

66. I am one who has power over serpents (Mark 16:18)

67. I am one who cannot be poisoned (Mark 16:18)

68. I am one who lays hands on the sick, so that they will recover (Mark 16:18)

69. I am one who loves (Gal. 5:22; 1 John 4:16)

70. I am one who has joy (Gal. 5:22; John 15:11)

71. I am one who has peace (Gal. 5:22; John 14:27)

72. I am one who has patience (Gal. 5:22)

73. I am one who has kindness (Gal. 5:22)

74. I am one who has goodness (Gal. 5:22)

75. I am one who has faith (Gal. 5:22)

76. I am one who has gentleness (Gal. 5:23)

77. I am one who has self-control (Gal. 5:23)

78. I am one who has all the fruit of the Spirit (Gal. 5:22, 23)

79. I am one who has the mind of Christ (1 Cor. 2:16)

80. I am led by the Spirit of God (Gal. 5:18)

81. I am chosen (1 Cor. 1:27, 28; James 2:5)

82. I am a disciple (John 8:31)

83. I am a priest (1 Peter 2:9; Rev. 1:6)

84. I am a king (Rev. 1:6)

85. I am an ambassador for Christ (1 Cor. 5:20)

86. I am an intercessor who stands in the gap (Ezek. 22:30)

87. I am a watchman on the wall (Ezek. 3:17)

88. I am baptized in the Holy Spirit (Acts 2:4)

89. I am endued with power from on high (Luke 24:49)

90. I am one who has overcome (1 John 4:4)

91. I am one who has been freely given all things through Christ (Rom. 8:32; 1 Cor. 3:21)

92. I am one who can do all things through Christ who strengthens me (Phil. 4:13)

93. I am one God always leads in triumph in Christ (2 Cor. 2:14)

94. I am one God gives the victory to through our Lord Jesus Christ (1 Cor. 15:57)

95. I am one who has within him the One who is greater than he that is in the world (1 John 4:4)

96. I am one who treads upon the lion and the cobra, the young lion and the serpent I trample underfoot (Ps. 91:13)

97. I am one who can run through a troop and leap over a wall (Ps. 18:29)

98. I am a soldier of Christ (2 Tim. 2:3-4)

99. I am a royal horse in the day of battle (Zech. 10:3)

100. I am fully armed with weapons that are mighty through God (2 Cor. 10:5)

101. I am more than a conqueror (Rom 8:37)

102. I am able to pull down strongholds (2 Cor. 10:5)

103. I am able to cast down imaginations and every high lofty thing that exalts itself against the knowledge of God (2 Cor. 10:5)

104. I am able to bring into captivity every thought (2 Cor. 10:5)

105. I am a stranger to this world, a pilgrim just passing through (Heb 11:13)

106. I am a witness (1 Thess. 2:10)

107. I am bold (2 Cor. 11:21)

108. I am the Bride of Jesus Christ (Rev. 21:2-10)

109. I am jealous for the saints with a godly jealousy. (2 Cor. 11:2)

110. I am a minister of the Gospel of Christ (2 Cor. 11:23; Rom. 1:16)

111. I am not my own (1 Cor. 6:19)

112. I am not of this world (John 15:9)

113. I am not under the law (Gal. 5:18)

114. I am not a slave (Gal. 4:7)

115. I am not inferior (Job 13:2)

116. I am not alone (John 8:16; 16:32)

117. I am not ashamed of the Gospel of Christ (Rom. 1:16)

118. I am not ashamed of who I am (2 Tim. 1:12)

119. I am what I am by the grace of God, and His grace toward me will not be in vain, I will labor more abundantly than anyone else by the grace of God which is with me (1 Cor. 15:10).

Appendix B compiled by Pastor Dale Howell, Cornerstone Church, Grants Pass, Oregon.

- NOTES -

- NOTES -

- NOTES -

- NOTES -

- NOTES -

Would you like to Host a *School of the Prophetic* with Ivan Roman in your Church or Region?

Visit www.afriendofgod.org for more Information

We're living in a time and season in which hearing God for ourselves is absolutely essential if we want our businesses to be blessed, our ministries to flourish, the nations to be taken, and even, in many cases, to receive revelation and direction for our family's survival and wellbeing. These are the days scribed by the prophet Joel: *"It will come about after this that I will pour out My Spirit on all mankind; and your sons and daughters will prophesy, your old men will dream dreams, and your young men will see visions"* (Joel 2:28-29). In this hour, God is pouring out His Spirit causing a prophetic generation to arise that will live in supernatural intimacy with the Lord—abiding in the heavens and bringing heaven to earth—ultimately ushering in the second coming of Christ!

In the *School of the Prophetic* you will receive foundational training and equipping that's essential for moving in the prophetic ministry! You'll learn to discern the voice of God on a greater level, get stretched and grow in your prophetic gift, and receive a fresh impartation of the revelatory gifts and anointings God wants to activate in your life! Are you hungry for fresh encounters in His presence? Do you believe God has something more for you than what you're currently walking in? Do you want an increase of dreams, visions, and heavenly encounters? If so, don't miss this school! You're about to step into a supernatural lifestyle you know you're called to deep inside. Whether you're a novice in the prophetic ministry or a seasoned prophet, if you're hungry for God and simply want more, this school is for you!

A Friend of God Ministries Presents:

Friend of God
Road Schools

School of
Identity & Authority

Instructor: Ivan Roman

Would you like to Host a *School of Identity* with Ivan Roman in your Church or Region?

Visit www.afriendofgod.org for more Information

In this hour the Lord is raising up an end time army that will shake the nations of the earth! This task force is made up of Spirit filled sons and daughters of God—a generation entirely sold out to fulfill the Kingdom Mandate and Great Commission: *On earth as it is in Heaven.* This will be a people who know their God and do great exploits!

In the *School of Identity and Authority,* the Spirit of God will unlock and release to you heavenly revelation and knowledge of *who* you are, *whose* you are, and *who lives inside of you!* Are you hungry for fresh encounters in His presence? Do you believe God has something more for you? If so, get ready for a paradigm shift that will change the way you see God, yourself, and everyone around you forever! God is longing to give you a fresh impartation of revelation and power—a fresh touch from heaven that will spill out everywhere you go! No more sitting on the sidelines—get ready to be activated in a supernatural lifestyle like never before!

Additional Copies of this manual
and other resources and training material
can be found at www.fusionbookstore.com
or by calling 1 (615) 542-8285.

Fusion Creations

P.O. Box 17412

Nashville, TN 37217

Made in the USA
Lexington, KY
07 April 2013